JUST ACROSS THE CHANNEL

Just Across The Channel

The best guide to daytrips, weekends and short holidays in nearest France

by

Charles Owen

CADOGAN BOOKS LTD

ISBN 0946313 008

Published by Cadogan Books Ltd 1983
15 Pont Street, London SW1

Typeset in Great Britain by
M.C. Typeset, Chatham, Kent
Printed and bound by
The Pitman Press

Acknowledgements

In writing this book I have enjoyed invaluable help and support from many quarters, first from Faith Hallett who, usually in London, sometimes in France, has been my head researcher, chief of staff and general right-hand person; and second from Jill Roper who, partly in France, mainly at my Devon home, besides helping with research, has borne the brunt of typing most of the text. The journeys, made for the book during 1982, gained also from preparation and on-the-spot fact-finding by, among others, Amanda Kent, Lorna Macleod, Teresa White and my son, Rupert.

Much of the data for Chapters 7, 9 and 10 was assembled by Faith Hallett. For most of the material on which Chapter 8 is based, I am indebted to art historians Marjorie Allthorpe-Guyton and Felicity, my wife, each of whom travelled specially to France, the former concentrating on Normandy. I also acknowledge advice or assistance from Virginia Graham, Jane Lingard, Susanne Purvis and Christine Waugh.

As for sources, I wrote in advance, to invite guidance and information, to a wide range of concerns including the ferry companies, a number of airline and coach operators offering destinations in northern France and to various representatives in England of special holiday interests. I wrote also to numerous regional and local tourist offices and chambers of trade throughout northern France. The response, if patchy, was invariably friendly, sometimes enthusiastic. At the risk of being invidious I must single out, for co-operation beyond the call of duty, the managements of the P & O and Sally Viking ferry companies; of the Chaîne Lucien Barrière hotel group and its member establishment, the Royal at Deauville; the Best Western hotel group, including its members, the Carlton at Lille and the

Dieppe at Rouen; and the directorates of the Seine Maritime and Dieppe tourist authorities.

* * * *

I recommend as companions indispensable to my readers, as they were to me, the *Michelin Green Guides for Nord/Pas de Calais, Normandy* and *Brittany*; the *Red Michelin Guide for France*; the *Thomas Cook Continental Timetable*; the French Tourist Office in London's reference booklet, *France*; the brochures/timetables of the cross-Channel ferry companies and the appropriate area Michelin road maps, scale 1cm:2km, for the region. The French Tourist Office in London also helped with tourist literature, as far as its own incomplete stocks allowed, supplementing the cascades of generally impressive leaflets and brochures which reached me through the post in response to my introductory letters to addresses in France.

* * * *

I found the following publications useful. As general guides: *Beating the Channel Crossing* by Frank Barratt (*Sunday Times Magazine*, 25 July 1982); *How to Win at Holidays Abroad* edited by Philip Clarke (*Sunday Times Magazine*, 4 January 1981); *France*, a Letts Guide, by Harold Dennis-Jones (Charles Letts, 1980); *Brittany and Normandy* by Mary Elsy (Batsford, 1974); *Traveller's France* by Arthur Epéron (Pan, 1979); *French Entrée* by Patricia Fenn (Quiller Press, 1982); *Guide des Hôtels, Logis et Auberges de France* (Firedit, Paris, 1981); *France's Normandy* by Brian Moore (*Travel and Leisure* magazine, June 1982); *Sixty Miles from England* by Simona Packenham (Macmillan, 1967); *The Companion Guide to Normandy* by Nesta Roberts (Collins, 1980); *Blue Guide to Loire Valley, Normandy and Brittany* edited by Ian Robertson (Ernest Benn, 1978); *Guide des Relais Routiers* (SEJT, Paris, 1982); *The North of France* by Frederick Tingey (Spurbooks, 1978).

On history: *A Concise History of France* by Marshall B.

Davidson (Cassell, 1972); *A Concise History of France* by Douglas Johnson (Thames and Hudson, 1971); *The Hundred Years' War* by Edouard Perroy (Eyre and Spottiswoode, 1965); *Dieppe 1942* by Ronald Atkin (Macmillan, 1980); *The First Day on the Somme* by Martin Middlebrook (Allan Lane, 1971).

On art and architecture: *Art and Architecture in France, 1500 to 1700* by Anthony Blunt (Pelican, 1953); *French XVIII Century Painters* by Edmond and Jules de Goncourt (Phaidon, 1948); *Watercolour Painting in Britain*, Vols II and III by Martin Hardie (Batsford, 1967, 1968); *A Dictionary of Art and Artists* by Peter and Linda Murray (Penguin, 1959); *John Sell Cotman: Normandy Drawings in Norwich Castle Museum* by Miklos Rajni and Marjorie Allthorpe-Guyton (Norfolk Museum Service, 1975); *Encyclopaedia of Impressionism* by Maurice Sérullaz (Phaidon, 1978).

CO

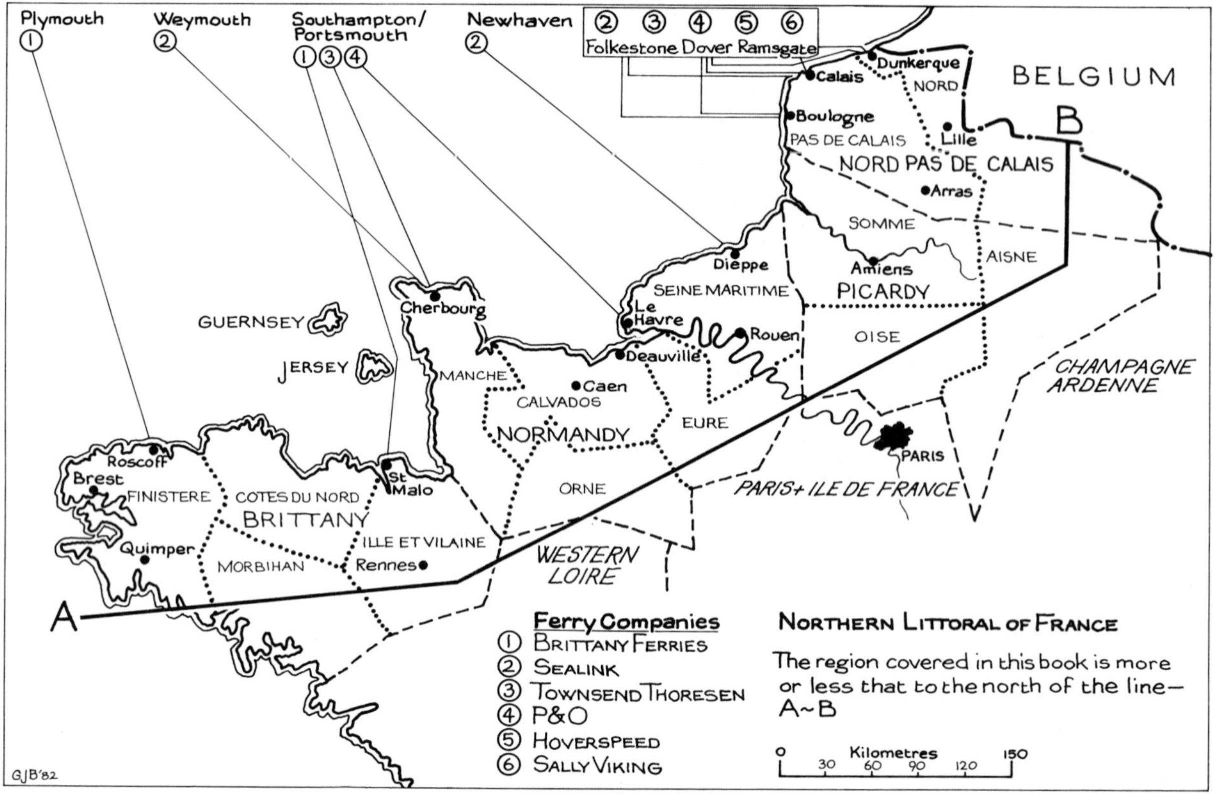

Ferry Companies

1. Brittany Ferries
2. Sealink
3. Townsend Thoresen
4. P&O
5. Hoverspeed
6. Sally Viking

Northern Littoral of France

The region covered in this book is more or less that to the north of the line— A~B

Contents

Preface
How to use the book

This book is about short holidays in northern France. It takes in almost the whole length of coastline from the Belgian frontier to Finisterre and inland places within about two hours' travelling time, by car or train, from the nearest French ferry ports. All the ports with regular services from England are featured: Dunkerque, Calais, Boulogne, Dieppe, Le Havre, Cherbourg, St Malo and Roscoff; and, besides numerous other resorts, Lille, Arras, Le Touquet, Amiens, Rouen, Deauville, Caen, Rennes, Dinard and Brest are among the major cities and well-known watering places which are included.

Between April and September 1982 I made several cross-Channel journeys specially for this book and a selection of these, in a condensed form, and divided into six chapters, is described in Parts One and Two. In each of them the reader accompanies the author along a particular route, sometimes by car, sometimes by public transport, and the author's journeys make use between them, one way or the other, as motorist or as foot passenger, of services operated by all these ferry companies : Sally Viking, Hoverspeed, Sealink, P & O, Townsend Thoresen and Brittany Ferries.

The duration of these journeys, apart from occasional options or variations, ranges from one to six days, but as these times include the ferry crossings, considered by many to be part of the holiday, the higher figure still falls within the limits of the motorist's five-day excursion as usually offered by the ferry companies.

To balance and supplement the geographical arrangement of these journeys, most of the places, sights and amenities mentioned in them are repeated in abbreviated gazetteer form in the alphabetical town index of the book. Maps showing the routes of the author's journeys are at the beginning of the relevant chapters.

The rest of the book brings together information about the region as a whole which, if presented journey by journey, would lead to duplication: how to get there, how to travel around, history, economics, heritage and scenery, food and drink, sport and entertainment.

A beginner to this subject is invited to pick whichever of the journeys seems most likely to appeal to him and, having worked through the selected chapter, to consult the gazetteer and, perhaps, according to his interests, one or other of the general information chapters. He may then like to have a go at the journey itself, taking this book with him as his guide. If he needs additional information I recommend the *Thomas Cook Continental Timetable*, which contains the timings of all the cross-Channel ferries and of all the trains and some of the buses to which reference is made in this book. The traveller should take also the relevant Michelin regional road maps, and that best general guide book of all, with its useful town plans, the *Michelin Green Guide* for the appropriate area.

Finally, I hope my readers will appreciate that the journeys, as described in this book, cover a lot of ground in a short time. I hope these act, not merely as trails to be followed literally, but as a prompt to more leisurely or more adventurous and further-reaching travels.

Introduction
On getting across, about and settled

Some Definitions

The northern France region covered by this book is divided into four provinces: Nord/Pas de Calais, Picardy, Normandy and Brittany; and each province is sub-divided into a number of departments, the names of which are shown in my map, Northern Littoral of France. As most Britons hardly know their Aisne from their Orne and are probably left cold by the difference, all this may seem a little far-fetched, but with France's official tourism organisation broken down that way it often helps to understand the local-government boundaries when consulting hotel lists or seeking information about districts beyond the confines of individual towns and cities.

French tourist literature is generally well written and presented, including illustrated leaflets covering every conceivable taste or interest. The French Tourist Office, (178 Piccadilly, London W1V 0AL) is the principal source in Britain of this material but, even if its stocks were complete at any given time, it could understandably respond to vague or ill-defined enquiries only with generalised information. If you hope for precise details you must know what you want. And, incidentally, beware of the growing tendency in tourist literature, not only France's, for items to be undated, old-stock leaflets and lists containing last year's prices being of little value.

The services and amenities mentioned in this book are (in 1982, were) available at least during the summer months: *In the case of public transport there may at any time be variations on weekend days, while some hotels, restaurants and institutions may open only for a limited season and, even then, be closed for a day or so each week.*

Getting There

The cross-Channel routes served by the ferry companies are summarised in Part A of Chapter 10. Most of these, naturally, are concentrated in the Straits of Dover. Quayside connections with trains are available on some services at Dover (Western Docks only, and rarely), Folkestone, Calais, Boulogne, Newhaven and Dieppe. One advantage of the routes to Le Havre, St Malo and Roscoff is that a full night's sleep may be enjoyed on the overnight services.

All ships and hovercraft are one class only. Hovercraft amenities are similar to those on short-haul aircraft. Frills apart, there is not a great deal to choose between the ships: all have shops with duty-free goods, bars, lounges, self-service catering; some have table-service restaurants, one-arm bandits, discos. In a crowded ship the effect of all this is often too many passengers standing around in queues and not enough space for the queues to stand around in. But cabins or berths are generally available: on overnight services advance booking is advisable; and most ships have the odd quiet corner, undiscovered by the more boisterous seagoing elements, of which school parties are the most tiresome. One ferry company Chairman writes that these groups 'are on occasion a great annoyance to our customers and an embarrassment to ourselves', this being 'a problem which we share with others in the industry and is of great concern to us'. Amen.

Other Tips

Vehicles do not necessarily disembark in the sequence in which they embarked. Foot passengers board sometimes by the car ramp, more usually by separate gangway, the walk from the terminal either way being unsheltered and often, for people with hand baggage, a pretty long way. Information for arriving foot passengers in the terminals about onward transportation may be sparse: local buses are sometimes available, the town centres, except for Boulogne and Dieppe, being quite a step from the ferry berths, although if travelling light in dry weather the distances are tolerable on foot in Le Havre (Townsend Thoresen only), Cherbourg and St Malo.

Until the Channel Tunnel arrives and puts the ferry companies on their mettle, the least irksome and most stress-free way to cross over into France is by ferry-borne motor coach. You are driven on board the vessel, the driver having coped with the embarkation rituals, and you can leave your baggage in the vehicle; on disembarkation your party will be on its way long before most of the cars that crossed with you; and if you are on an inclusive tour the coach and its driver or courier will remain at your disposal. Of course, this cossetted, pre-planned way of seeing the world may seem too restricting to motorists and other independently minded travellers, but even for them, when considering the short one-day trip across the Channel for just lunch and shopping, there is much to be said in terms of cost and convenience for joining or making up a coach party.

The ferry companies can usually tell you which coach operators are in this line of business and, for that matter, which are offering longer-distance tours and holidays. Deservedly, this form of travel is growing fast and it may be well worth shopping around for a tour to suit both your interests and your pocket. For information about this as well as other means of travel to northern France the reference booklet, 'France', issued by the French Tourist Office in London, has useful lists of carriers; and no doubt your local travel agent can make suggestions.

The biggest puzzle for the cross-Channeller is that posed by the competing ferry companies' variable fares structures and timetables. From Dover, with its concentration of frequent services, why not a standard fare and interchangeable tickets valid on the next or any sailing, space permitting, regardless of the company operating it? As it is, the ships and hovercraft between them ply regularly from England to France along some fifteen routes, vying with each other, not least with their 'bargain' short-period return fares for motorists on the one hand and foot passengers on the other, allowing between one and five days on the Continent. As fares may vary according to company, route, season, day of week, time of day or night, duration of stay, whether part of a package, type of on-board accommodation and length of car, the brochures make complicated reading.

However, these brochures may offer information not only about their own prices, timings and conditions of travel but on where to go and where to stay in the areas to which their services give access.

On prices: in 1982 the ordinary return fare for a small family car and two adults ranged from £56 off-peak Dover–Calais to £210 high season Portsmouth–St Malo, or from £41 Dover–Calais to £125 Portsmouth–St Malo for a 5-day return; while for foot passengers the fare ranged from £5 for a day return Ramsgate–Dunkerque to £40 for an ordinary return Plymouth–Roscoff.

Anyone reluctant to sort all this out for himself should seek skilled advice: among the best informed travel agents, Ferrysave offer a clear and comprehensive catalogue with choice of prices, including in their case insurance for both vehicle and passengers.

There are various cross-Channel air services but none nowadays which carries cars; and it is more expensive by air than by sea to nearest France. In Chapter 10 I list the airports of places mentioned in this book where these have direct air services from England: most run only or mainly in the summer, the principal carriers being Air France, Britair, Brymon and Touraine.

Getting About on The Other Side

If not encumbered with baggage the jolliest way to get close to the French people and their way of life, while yourself making useful progress from A to B, is by public transport. Local and cross-country timetables or prompt and reliable oral information about services are not all that easy to come by, most tourist offices and bus depots being oddly reticent about such mundane matters. But if your French is not too halting, your questions are not too vague, the day is not too hot and the queues are not too long, railway enquiry staffs can be very obliging.

To help surmount the obstacles and encourage the adventurous tourist I have whenever possible in this book made a feature of *rail travel.* I avoid giving exact train times because these may change, although usually only marginally if at all, year by year: instead I use terms such as 'mid morning' or 'late evening' to denote services which, in 1982, as I know from careful checks or personal experience, ran accordingly. This apart, as I mention elsewhere, a copy of the *Thomas Cook Continental Timetable* is all you need to navigate yourself around northern France by train and, between whiles, to master the rail enthusiast's substitute for every man's crossword puzzle.

In case you are a stranger to French Railways: most stations in France are rather grander and tidier than Britain's, and the passengers treat their trains like extensions of their homes. Cleanliness is appreciated, sticky post-prandial debris is not usually left for the next occupant, before putting a foot on the opposite seat the dirty shoe is removed or rested on a newspaper; and, while most trains are air-conditioned, windows in the rest remain closed when under way so that the other passengers are not exposed to draughts. In main line trains without a restaurant or buffet car refreshments are often available off a trolley wheeled air-liner style right through the train. The proportion of first- to second-class accommodation tends to be greater on French than British trains and, reflecting a higher productivity achieved partly by a lower frequency of services, both classes are normally fuller.

At the principal stations Access or Visa credit cards are accepted as payment for tickets. Platforms are open and before boarding his train each passenger must punch his own ticket in one of the machines provided for this purpose: failing this a fine may be imposed by the ticket inspector en route. Ordinary fares seem to be a little lower than those in Britain but there is a comparative lack of 'bargain' tickets such as Awaydays, Savers and so on. If you expect to travel fairly widely by train, however, it might be wise before leaving England to buy a tourist's Rover ticket or, if you are eligible, a reduced-fare family, couple or pensioner's rail card: ask French Railways, whose London Office, (179 Piccadilly, W1V 0BA), is next door to the French Tourist Office.

In most French towns and cities the main bus station adjoins the main rail station. *Bus services* are generally less frequent and extensive than in Britain and bus stops are usually further apart. You can buy your ticket from the driver when you enter his bus, remembering that he might be less good-tempered than his British counterpart in giving change, and if ticket vending machines are available at the boarding point he may wonder protestingly why you failed to make use of them. On country buses the driver will often exchange barbed wit over his shoulder with his passengers but, with other road users generally giving French bus drivers a wide berth, no one gets hurt. Even so, if you have a choice I recommend the train.

For personal transport: if you leave your own car in England, *car and bicycle hire* are widely available. Do not assume, however, that it will necessarily be made easy for you to park your own car close to the ferry berth at the port of departure: in some cases, having found a secure park with reasonable charges, a walk of up to half a mile may be involved, with no baggage trolleys to help you. For hire cars in France the weekend is usually lower than the mid-week rate: in summer 1982 a well-known company was quoting less than £20 for a Renault 5 with unlimited mileage (though you buy your own petrol as you go) from Friday afternoon to Monday morning.

In northern France bicycles may be hired at the main rail stations in Argentan, Bayeux, Caen, Calais, Deauville, Dieppe, Dinan, Dinard, Dives, Granville, Guingamp, Lannion, Morlaix, Roscoff, St Brieuc and St Malo, the rate in 1982 being about £2 a day including insurance, rear luggage rack, lights and everything you need except someone to push you up the hills.

Sleeping it Off

In grading and pricing *hotels* I have adopted the star system used in Britain by the AA and RAC. This is akin to the French official system, applicable to all hotel lists issued over there by the tourist authorities, except that their top category, equivalent to Britain's *****, is ****L. Hotel prices in France relate more to the quality of the room than to the number of occupants or to the class of hotel, and a spacious, well-furnished room with private facilities in, say, a 2-star hotel may cost much the same as similar accommodation in, say, a 3-star hotel. In summer 1982 such a room, twin-bedded, was priced more or less between 150 F and 250 F, service and tax included, although the cheapest rate in a 2-star hotel for a room without private bath and WC could be as low as 80 F.

Except that, with sound logic, the luxury ***** (or ****L) grade is considered inapplicable, *camps* are starred the same way as hotels from **** 'very comfortable, low-density sites with comprehensive amenities where great care is taken with landscaping' to * 'amenities are fairly basic but adequate'. A free leaflet giving full information about *camping and caravanning* facilities is available for each province: as these indicate, and as a visit will confirm, sites are plentiful, standards high and amenities often comprehensive enough for the camper to find everything he needs for his holiday on the spot, as a general rule the inland camps being better cared for than those on the coast. One indication of price: in early summer 1982 a family of four travelling by Dormobile in Brittany was paying between £3 and £6 a night, according to the camp's quality and location.

In France, as in Britain, *self-catering* in all its forms is a fast-growing industry although holiday flats in resorts seem to be less widely or readily available: the local tourist office can advise you. The furnished country cottage or 'gîte', increasingly popular with Britons, is becoming more and more prevalent: Brittany Ferries, active in this market, were making it possible in 1982 for a party of four to enjoy a week in a gîte from about £45 a head including a return ticket for the car.

The extensive waterways of Brittany are well known to visitors wishing to base their holidays on *hired barges or motor cruisers*. But if the wind is fair and your crew willing the cheapest way of all to go to nearest France is in your own yacht, the whole of that region being well endowed with attractive anchorages and well-run marinas.

Whatever your choice of craft, *bon voyage, bonnes vacances et surtout, bon appétit*!

Author's Journeys : North-East France, Brittany and Normandy

Chapter 1 : Beaten Track

Summary

After a Sunday outing to Boulogne for lunch, we set off again from Dover with a P & O 48-hour return to explore the Boulogne area more fully, thus:

Day	*With Car*
1st	Mid-afternoon, arrive **Boulogne** from Dover. Take direct route south (D940) avoiding town centre. Divert to Hardelot.
	Arrive **Le Touquet** early evening. Tour town, select hotel, check in. (*Rec*: Westminster or Côte D'Opale.) Walk-about, choose restaurant for dinner. (*Rec*: L'Orée.)
2nd	Early start. Continue south. Divert to Berck and St Valéry-sur-Somme. Pause briefly in **Abbeville.**
	Proceed north (D928) to Hesdin and west (N39) to **Montreuil.** Lunch. (*Rec*: Château, appetite and purse permitting, or Darnetal brasserie.) After visit to castle and walkabout, return to Le Touquet. Tour ourskirts and settle for dinner. (*Rec*: L'Escale, at the airport.)
3rd	Final walk or jog in Le Touquet. Leave mid-morning by inland routes via the Boulonnais countryside to **Wimereux.** Walkabout, shop, lunch. (*Rec*: L'Atlantic.)

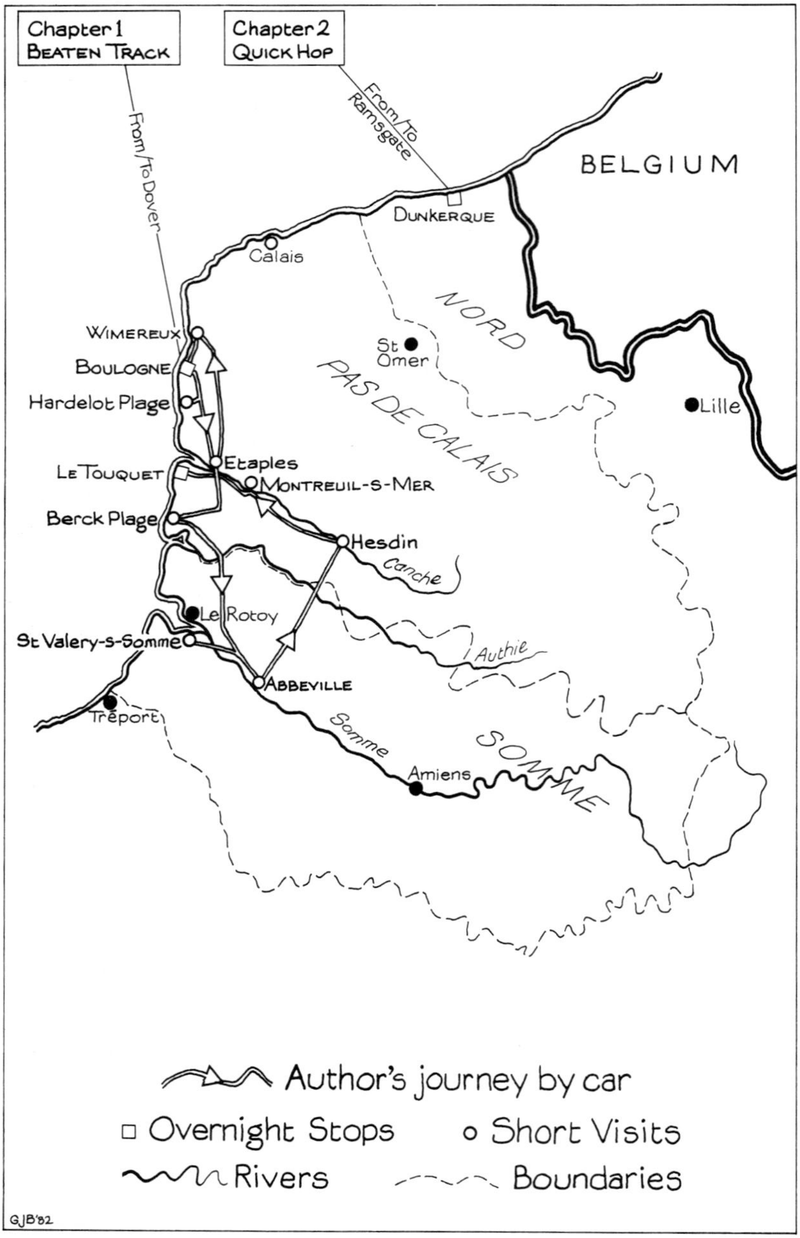
Chapter 1
Beaten Track
Chapter 2
Quick Hop
From/To Dover
From/To Ramsgate
BELGIUM
Dunkerque
Calais
NORD
Wimereux
St Omer
Boulogne
PAS DE CALAIS
Hardelot Plage
Lille
Etaples
Le Touquet
Montreuil-s-Mer
Berck Plage
Hesdin
Canche
Le Rotoy
St Valery-s-Somme
Authie
Abbeville
Tréport
Somme
SOMME
Amiens
Author's journey by car
Overnight Stops
Short Visits
Rivers
Boundaries
GJB'82

Continue to Boulogne. See Haute Ville, walkabout Basse Ville. Shop. Early evening, embark for Dover.

Day *Without Car*

1st

Mid-afternoon, arrive **Boulogne** from Dover. Select hotel, check in. (*Rec*: Alexandra, Faidherbe, Métropole.) Walkabout in Haute Ville, then choose restaurant for dinner. (*Rec*: Welsh Pub, unless one of the Haute Ville bistros tempts you.)

2nd Early start. Bus to **Le Touquet.** Walkabout.

Late morning. Bus or taxi to Etaples, thence train to **Montreuil.** Lunch. (*Rec*: Château, appetite and purse permitting, or Darnetal brasserie.) Visit castle, walkabout.

Early evening. Bus or train to Boulogne. Select district for dinner, eg beach-harbour area. (*Rec*: La Matelote or La Plage.)

3rd Bus or train to **Wimereux.** Walkabout, Lunch. (*Rec*: L'Atlantic.)

Bus to Boulogne. Shop. Early evening, embark for Dover.

Author's Narrative

Most Britons disembarking in **Boulogne** are in a hurry. They aim to continue south by road or railway, avoiding the town, and a glimpse of its pleasure beach and casino as they enter the harbour is not really enough to offset the forbidding post-war architecture forming the town's frontage on the far side of the river Liane, main artery of Boulogne's extensive harbour.

Half a century ago, before the destruction wreaked by World

War II, the nearest part of the town, the Basse Ville, was picturesque enough to entice a visitor over the Pont Marguet and into its heart. At that time, Boulogne was still described as 'a popular and gay watering-place, with a considerable English colony', and its main raison d'être as a tough, hard-working industrial and fishing community was played down. Nowadays, besides its ever-growing success as a short-stay tourist resort, Boulogne is happy to flex its muscles not only as France's second passenger port but as its largest fishing port, a substantial commercial port and the home of several forms of heavy and light manufacturing industry.

The Gare Maritime at Boulogne, served by Sealink ferries from Dover and Folkestone and by P & O Ferries from Dover, is within a short walk of the town centre, and just across the bridge, at the approach to Rue Faidherbe, is the tourist office. In the summer some Sealink ferries connect on the quayside with trains to Paris and beyond, while at other times a bus connects the Gare Maritime with Boulogne-Ville station. The modern hoverport, handling Hoverspeed hovercraft from Dover, is over a mile from the centre of Boulogne but has its own rail station with connecting fast trains to Paris and a bus into Boulogne.

Motorists going further afield are routed clear of central Boulogne but the first stage, in company with the heavy lorries, is through unattractive built-up districts. It takes a little longer and more careful driving to exit through the town but this way is more interesting.

The British have long been the most numerous among foreigners in these parts. In the 18th century some of those with financial misfortunes in England found life more tolerable just across the Channel, and by the 19th century, in the prosperity following Napoleon's fall, many more flocked across, some to enjoy the first thermal baths in Europe and others the new fashion of sea bathing from the long sandy beach. The search for a refuge remained: at one time, the population of the prison was so overwhelmingly British, all incarcerated for debt, that it came to be known as the Hôtel d'Angleterre.

But the Briton has often landed here with a more belligerent intent, from the days of the battles of Crecy and Agincourt, the campaigns of World Wars I and II, to the present era when, from time to time, a ferry load of bargain-hunting day trippers, their skins full of heady plonk, leave their mark in broken heads and beaten-up cafés: in the eyes of the Boulonnais, presumably, a fair price to pay for the money flowing their way from that uncouth country the other side of La Manche.

However, the mass of British tourists come peacefully and politely enough, gingerly tenant à droit in their trim GB-plated cars as they start their southward journeys or, phrasebook in hand, sampling carefully some of the pleasures and pitfalls of this nearest piece of France; and they are over there in their droves and growing numbers thanks largely to the proliferating services and bargain fares of the several cross-Channel ferry companies serving the Côte d'Opale ports of Boulogne, Calais and Dunkerque.

*   *   *   *

Sunday Outing

Boulogne, with nearby Wimereux (5 kilometres to the north), makes an ideal destination for anyone from London or south-east England wanting to cross to France for lunch; and Sunday is an ideal day for this outing. No need to take the car: most Boulogne restaurants are near the port, and Wimereux is served by regular buses from the town centre. If, instead, you would like door-to-door transport there are several inexpensive there-and-back coach services, with stops at a pre-selected restaurant and hypermarket plus a quick sightseeing tour. If no such arrangement serves your district you can easily form your own party and ask Hoverspeed to fix the details.

As you land in Boulogne around lunchtime the contrast with London is exhilarating. In England on Sunday morning the streets are deserted and, except for a two-hour period in the middle of the day when the pubs are open, and a few rather subdued eating places, mainly in the hotels, there is nowhere to eat and drink, let alone be merry. But in Boulogne everyone is cheerfully and energetically out and about. The cafés and restaurants and many shops are trading briskly, the streets are bursting at their seams; and as elsewhere in France people sit where they can be seen, to eat and be convivial, served by smartly turned out waiters, and passing crowds being all part of the entertainment.

When I last went there for lunch, on a hot windless summer Sunday, the mid-morning Sealink ferry from Folkestone, reached by connecting train from Victoria, was not too full. Between spells on deck it was a pleasure to sit in the bar, a duty-free drink in hand, and read the Sunday papers.

Ashore in Boulogne, the pavement cafés and souvenir shops of Rue Faidherbe were doing capacity business and so, apparently, were the restaurants in the market square, Place Dalton. As I walked slowly past, reading their menus, a couple, having lunched early, vacated a table by a wide open window overlooking the square. I hurried between the tables on the pavement, up a few steps and into a bustling brasserie with its unique French aroma of garlic-spiced food. *Le patron*, following my gaze, led me to the desired table which, already cleared, was being relaid on a crisp white tablecloth; and as my companion and I settled on the bench seat beside the window and received the menu, a French family next to us smiled good morning, enquired after the English weather and wished us '*bon appétit*'.

The lunch, with a main course of fish in a *piquant* sauce, was excellent, and by the time we had done justice to it and the house wine, the restaurant was almost empty. I paid the bill and shook our host's hand and we went into the square. 'I must make a note of that place,' I said as we walked away. My companion laughed, as well she might: for the name of that admirable French eating place was, incongruously, The Welsh Pub.

With a couple of hours before check-in for our return ferry we decided to visit the upper part of the town, the Haute Ville. As we climbed slowly under the blazing sun the crowds thinned. Houses and flats lay tranquil in the heat, their windows open and their occupants, presumably, at their siesta. The old hill-top ramparts containing the castle, town hall, Notre Dame cathedral and the narrow cobbled streets flanked by several small, inviting bistros and cafés, offered both a haven of peace and a reminder that Boulogne, dating from Roman times, has always been strategically important.

Fortified by Errard in the 13th century (some of the early ramparts are still intact) and by Vauban in the 17th, Boulogne had special links with Napoleon, who assembled an enormous army there with a view to invading England. In the process he enlarged the port to accommodate 2,000 ships. In 1940 Hitler, with equal lack of success, tried much the same again. These predatory gentlemen foolishly ignored the firm sentiments expressed by a plaque dated 1671, displayed prominently in Boulogne's museum, thus: 'France and England well united could defy all the World'.

* * * *

The Two-Day Trip

More recently I drove to the admirably well-run car ferry terminal at Dover's Eastern Docks and, having bought a 48-hour 'Cheepie' return ticket for the car and two of us, was ushered straight on board P & O's *Tiger*, which was soon en route for Boulogne. The object of this trip was to sample scenery and resorts around Boulogne and up to 100 kilometres to the south and east and, in the same area, to identify a few recommended restaurants, including some with a Michelin Guide rosette.

Le Touquet made an excellent centre for this journey. After a short drive, mainly through industrial suburbs and, briefly, along the undistinguished riverside at Etaples, we found ourselves in the well-manicured approaches to what the *Blue Guide to North-Eastern France* of 1930 used to describe as a 'highly fashionable' and 'expensive' resort. Le Touquet, known also as Paris-Plage, still retains, in places, an opulent ease, a reminder of its once-envied role as a chic rendezvous for smart-set personalities, including an uppercrust conspicuous for its tweedy clothes and Old Etonian accents. For Le Touquet owes its origins mainly to wealthy English people determined to create a stylish and exclusive foreign retreat as near to England as you can get it, to indulge there in gambling, golf, gastronomy, *thés dansants* and cocktail parties.

The town of Le Touquet lies snugly on level ground beside the mouth of the Canche estuary between a large forest, planted over a century ago to protect the newly-built villas from the wind and the sea, and an exceptionally wide, firm, sandy beach. The approach from Etaples through the trees, after skirting the golf courses, is by way of what remains of the elegant quarter, with its fine casino building, boulevard, villas and terraces of smart, Paris-style shops and restaurants. In this enclave is the imposing old-established 4-star Westminster Hotel, its rear looking across the gardens of some of the more spectacular villas towards the lighthouse; and close by is Flavio, the most sophisticated restaurant in this corner of France with its Michelin rosette, high prices and rather suave ambience. More suited to my pocket were L'Orée (next door) and, best buy of all, the gregarious and even more modestly-priced L'Escale brasserie and restaurant at Le Touquet airport, which is ignored by most tourists and, accordingly, much-favoured by the French.

The main part of the town, a compact grid of lively parallel streets, adjoins the snob area and offers a more everyday welcome to the visitor. Here, inland and on the seafront, are several small and unpretentious hotels, of which the 3-star Côte d'Opale and the 2-star Plage, both facing the sea, and the 3-star Manoir (2 kilometres inland near the *three* golf courses) are quieter and less claustrophobic than most. Half a mile to the south, at the end of the built-up area, right on the beach, is the modern 4-star Thalamer, a Continental-style health-resort hotel with its own tempting restaurant and swimming pool and the latest sports equipment and beauty salon.

On the beach and behind it Le Touquet caters lavishly for the visitor interested in sport. Besides golf courses it has numerous facilities for swimming, tennis, riding and sand yachting. It offers enough sheltered amenities to be tolerable even in poor weather; and the extensive beach itself, backed by rolling dunes and, often, by forests, stretches for several kilometres. The flat landscape and, to seaward, the high northern sky have a quality to inspire the poet and the artist.

If Le Touquet is the jewel of the **Côte d'Opale** the smaller neighbouring resorts, to judge by **Berck** and **Hardelot**, are less impressive, their former villagey charm somewhat spoiled by ugly blocks of flats and holiday homes. But Berck-Plage became a health resort during the last century after a fisherman's widow took in eight sick children and allowed them to play on the beach with astonishing results. Even today Berck has extremely bracing fresh air, its air being said to have only 4 bacteria per cubic metre compared with 900,000 in Paris; while Hardelot aptly describes itself as '*un Grand Jardin près de la Mer*'.

*   *   *   *

Woods, Views and Rivers

In general, the coast and its immediate hinterland give the arriving traveller an impression of a rather bleak and windswept landscape, but persevere for, inland, there is a pleasant variety of fertile country with small forests, hills, escarpments and river valleys.

Le Boulonnais, the mixed rolling farming countryside behind Boulogne, is unexpectedly pretty: wooded and with small, hidden valleys nestling in the hills. One 20-kilometre drive also takes in Wimereux and, on Boulogne's outskirts, the marble

Colonne de la Grande Armée, which was built to commemorate Napoleon's Camp du Boulogne. There are 263 steps to the top, and from there you can enjoy spectacular views of the sea to England, Cap Gris Nez, the port at Boulogne and the surrounding countryside.

A rather longer drive (about 80 kilometres) goes among the Boulonnais hills through tiny, picturesque villages like La Waast, Surques with its fortified church, and Questrecques. The forest of Boulogne is criss-crossed by marked footpaths and has clearings with picnic tables and benches while, on the other side of the River Liane, lies the more impressive Forest of Desvres.

On the other side of the Canche estuary from Le Touquet at Etaples, with its railway links to Paris, Lille and Boulogne, is an important British military cemetery containing the tombs of men who died at a nearby hospital in 1914–18. Further upstream, the Canche and its tributary, the Ternoise, wander their way peacefully through unspoiled valleys, their waters providing unsurpassable trout fishing. On the north bank of the Canche is the basket-weaving village of Marles, while opposite is Brimeux where the old Roman road from Lyon to Boulogne crossed this river, and nearby is Beaurainville where Harold of England was held prisoner after being shipwrecked in 1064.

Further east, in largely re-built **Hesdin** the enormous Place d'Armes is still surrounded by 16th-century buildings, including the ornate Town Hall, a former royal palace, and the nearby Notre Dame church's doorway offers a fine example of Renaissance architecture.

On the far side of the Forest of Hesdin is the tiny hamlet of **Azincourt** (alias Agincourt) which, in 1415, saw one of the bloodiest battles of English history, where a small, exhausted English army of 6,000 archers led by Henry V, defeated 12,000 French opponents, mounted and on foot, and wiped out more than a hundred princes and noblemen.

The Authie valley, which marks the border with Picardy, is also worth exploring: like its better known neighbour, the

Somme, the river estuary is filled with wildfowl. At the mouth of the Somme, stranded by the easterly drift of sand that has helped to create the dunes along this coast, lies the former seaport of **St Valéry** from which William the Conqueror eventually set sail in 1066 for his invasion of England. A guardian, with Le Crotoy on the opposite bank, of the Somme estuary against attack, St Valéry was frequently under siege from one source or another for centuries: by the Vikings, by the English during the 100 Years' War, by the Spanish troops of Charles of Austria and, in turn, by the Catholics and Huguenots during the Wars of the League. But, despite its stormy past, St Valéry retains a number of old buildings, including solid fortifications with two massive gates and the 15th-century church of St Martin, and there are fine seaward and estuary views.

Of special interest is the reclaimed coastal area, mainly between the lower reaches of the Canche and Somme, known as **Marquenterre.** Like East Anglia, this is flat country intersected by waterways which have prevented the imposition of a coastal road, leaving the littoral largely under-developed and former sea-served communities, such as Montreuil and Abbeville, high and dry. Some 5,000 acres along the northern edge of the Somme estuary are now an important bird sanctuary, with marked paths among the dunes, lakes and marshes, and observation hides for watchers and photographers.

In 1272 Eleanor of Castile married Edward I in **Abbeville** and this prosperous trading town became British for 200 years. It continued to flourish until the 18th century when the receding sea and lessening demand for textiles caused a decline in its fortunes. In 1940, the Germans almost annihilated Abbeville with their bombs, causing a fierce reaction which did much to fuel the fire of Resistance fighters. The town has been almost entirely rebuilt in rather gloomy style and few of the old buildings survive.

* * * *

Montreuil Visit

We had reached **Montreuil** from Le Touquet on the second day of our trip, after a sweep southward close to the coast, a glimpse of the Somme estuary from St Valéry-sur-Somme, a northward circuit through Abbeville and Hesdin, and thence westward down the Canche valley. Here we found a small, walled market town, with old houses lining narrow streets radiating out from homely squares, a fine castle with sweeping views of the countryside from its ramparts and an ancient church, the whole steeped in history yet full of present-day bustle: a kind of up-dated fairy tale.

In this part of France, where war has erased so much of the past, Montreuil-sur-mer, with its 16th- and 17th-century streets, is the more a remarkable and cherished survival. But this is no backwater: despite its relaxed mood, it has always been in the centre of life. And of death, too, for here in the castle during World War I was the headquarters of Douglas Haig, Commander of the British forces, and a statue of him stands in Grand Place.

Below Montreuil flows the Canche and skirting it is the N1, the old-established main highway to Paris. Beside it stands its station on the railway from Boulogne to Lille; and it was once a leading port. Montreuil has been likened to Rye but it has more punch than Rye. It is more like a miniature of Lewes: brisk, worldly and purposeful, it suffers from a little too much traffic; and it has a tasteless tourist device in the castle grounds where, in return for a coin in the slot, a recorded commentary blares out from loudspeakers in the treetops, a crude substitute for the quieter human guides.

As for good living, at the approaches to the castle, hiding staidly behind its own high walls, is the distinguished 4-star Château de Montreuil hotel with its well-known restaurant, a sign of approval by today's affluent Britons being the Jaguars and Rovers parked outside. But less 'pricey' cafés and brasseries abound, of which the Darnetal attracted me, and the 2-star Central Hotel offers a warm welcome to the overnight visitor. Among other good things I found a bank open, and willing to change money, on a Saturday afternoon.

* * * *

Wimereux and Home

After Montreuil we drove the few kilometres back by the direct route to Le Touquet, which we explored further before dining at the airport restaurant; and next morning, on our third and final day, we set off by inland roads skirting Boulogne to **Wimereux**, a small, picturesque coastal town, fishing port and resort which proved to be a delight. You can walk around most of it in a few minutes, sensing a happy and prosperous community, with all its necessary amenities in convenient juxtaposition. Right on the beach, yet central, is the admirable L'Atlantic hostelry combining 3-star hotel, bar, brasserie and restaurant. Inside or at its tables on the edge of the beach you have a commanding view of the approaches to Boulogne harbour and, in the distance on a clear day, the cliffs of Dover.

The beach itself is a playground and, in particular, an exposed launching pad for the intrepid local yachtsmen. The restaurant on the first floor, with its Michelin rosette, run with verve and style, specialises in seafood and, naturally, is more highly priced than the brasserie and bar below: between them there is something for all tastes and pockets and, always, a flow of chattering people, L'Atlantic being a meeting place of the town as well as a tourist destination. A speciality of the house is its prizewinning cocktail 'Atlantic' which is made as follows:

> 'Dans une flute à champagne décorée de sucre cristalisé: 1 trait Cointreau, 2 traits Bitter Campari, 1 Cerise piquée dans un stick de bois, 1 paille. Remplir de champagne brut glacé.'

Before sampling the delights of L'Atlantic, we took the

opportunity to do some useful shopping in Wimereux in the local Co-op supermarket and, after lunch, we drove into Boulogne, with some two hours to spare before our ferry. This left time for a brief tour of the town, the upper part by car and the lower part on foot, and for a final foray into the shops. Boulogne is well equipped for shoppers, most of what you want being in or near the centre of the town including Champion, Prisunic and Monoprix supermarkets, while 4 kilometres along the road to Lille is the large Auchun hypermarket. There are also excellent town markets on Wednesdays and Saturdays in Place Dalton.

* * * *

Look, No Car

Do you have to take your car? By no means. Take your bike or hire one locally: most of this area is fairly flat and the distances are not too great. But public transport can serve you well if you make Boulogne your base, instead of Le Touquet, and you accept that you limit your chance of exploring the coastline and countryside.

In this case, on arrival in Boulogne check in at one of the town-centre hotels. Among those at 2-star level the Alexandra, Faidherbe and Métropole are pleasant and convenient. Each is within a few minutes' walk of all your local needs, including the rail and bus stations. And for dinner that first evening, after a walkabout including the Haute Ville, you might consider my homely friend, the Welsh Pub.

Next morning, leaving your luggage behind you, set off early by direct bus to Le Touquet. After two or three hours exploring that resort, proceed by bus or taxi to Etaples and there take the train for Montreuil, arriving just in time for lunch. Enjoy a healthy afternoon's walk in the town and its environs and in the early evening take the bus or train back to Boulogne. You could then try another quarter of that town, perhaps the beach and harbour area, where La Matelote, with its Michelin rosette, and

La Plage are among the restaurants that might interest you.

On your third and final morning, take a bus or train to Wimereux and, after a thorough walkabout, repair to L'Atlantic for your beach-side lunch. Thence, back to Boulogne by bus for final shopping and, having collected your baggage at the hotel, to the embarkation jetty for the voyage home.

Chapter 2 : Quick Hop

Author's Narrative

Diary Day 1

0745 Warm sunny morning as we leave London by car, and forecast on radio promises calm crossing to France: destination DUNKERQUE.

0842 Join M2 and work up to 60 knots course SSE, gaining good height crossing Medway.

0905 Steer into A299 and follow all navigation signs for Ramsgate, speed of advance 35 knots. Prepare charts for Ramsgate and tickets for ferry embarkation.

0940 After tedious approach to channel, reach Ramsgate harbour. Attractive terraces, meandering holiday makers, all basking in the sun. Impressive yacht marina. Turn right for Finnish-owned Sally Viking's departure berth.

0945 Check in at entrance gate for 1030 sailing. Glad to be in car having overtaken many foot passengers on long approach road, even entrance gate quite a step from terminal building, and terminal building quite a step from ferry gangway: foot passengers advised to avoid wet days and heavy hand baggage.

0950 We join squadrons of vehicles in large open space and settle down to a wait. Staff everywhere but no information offered though gather that ship now berthing is today's substitute for normal Sally Viking vessel.

1010 Disembarkation from ship in full swing, homeward cars passing us slowly to starboard. Waiting vehicles now include double decker buses on trans-world expedition, some heavy lorries, a few towed caravans, and heavily packed cars.

1020 The cohorts of foot-sloggers emerge from barrack-like

terminal annex and trudge slowly to boarding ramp. Loading of vehicles also begins, heavies first.

1050 As we approach we notice ship is Swedish and called *Prinsessan Desirée:* we hope trip will fulfil this name's exotic promise. We go aboard to be marshalled efficiently into our slots.

1055 Quick reconnaissance shows almost all seats in public rooms and passage ways and on large deck spaces already taken: on a wet day, standing room only? Dirty ashtrays and other debris from previous voyage. Long continuous queues for cafeteria, bar, restaurant, shop. Ship well equipped with dance floors: hard lying for refugees? Passengers all very orderly including many families with young children, plus areas of unusual silence due to large deaf and dumb party enjoying outing to France.

1110 Forty minutes late, *Desirée* picks up her petticoats, prepares to leave Ramsgate. Very slow exit: it is low tide, there is dredger in channel, not much water under Princess's bottom.

1115 At sea at last, 3½ hours after leaving central London: average speed so far barely 20 knots.

1430 French time (1330 English time). We pass through breakwaters into vast modern harbour of Dunkerque: endless lunar landscape, featureless expanses of docks, warehouses, alternating with huge industrial installations. Nothing man makes could be much uglier but economically worthwhile as Dunkerque is France's third largest port; it handles the latest in ocean-going transports, giant tankers, container ships, specialised cargo vessels of all kinds, and is doing well. Room for us, too: Sally Viking billet is plain quayside with simple industrialised terminal buildings.

1440 Berthing is swift and efficient: for once, having loaded through the stern at Ramsgate, we shall drive straight off here through the bows. But first, the hordes of foot passengers pour ashore through side of ship, down gangways, through bows, along car unloading ramp: fleet of motor coaches awaits them, their fate said to be a day's shopping and eating in Dunkerque before returning home this evening.

1500 We drive ashore: it is mid-afternoon in France, we are still miles short of Dunkerque itself, but only one passport officer is on car duty, and we must toe the line.

1515 Free at last, we head parallel to dockland, through endless empty acres of bleak duney desert, towards town. Until outskirts, no shops, no houses, no bars or cafés: oddly dispiriting even on this fine sunny day.

1540 We enter huge city, find Place de la République, secure head and stern by a parking meter and ring off main engines.

* * * *

First impressions of central **Dunkerque** were not encouraging. Extensively rebuilt since the war the streets seemed shapeless, the buildings all over the place, the traffic everywhere. Some of Dunkerque's windows seem to have suffered an epidemic of yellow frosted glass. And in the process of reconstruction, the town has managed to dampen the usual French animation and outdoor conviviality: or so it appeared to us as we set about finding our feet that afternoon.

But Dunkerque has much to offer the short-stay visitor, and in recent years, thanks largely to Sally Viking's cheap fares policy, it has become one of the busiest destinations for British day trippers. A typical all-in itinerary might include a visit to a Dunkerque hypermarket, a tour of coastal Flanders and, maybe, either lunch with ¼ litre of wine in an out-of-town restaurant or a three-course meal in the homeward ship. Some of these trips are just organised lunch parties while others, having dropped their clients in the centre of Dunkerque, set them free for a few hours before taking them back to the ferry for the homeward voyage. In 1982 there-and-back prices for these trips from the Ramsgate area ranged from £5 to £19.

This route compared with the competition is also a bargain for motorists, and Dunkerque is a convenient port of entry for many parts of the Continent, with autoroutes for Paris, Lille, Belgium and the Rhineland starting nearby. One way to approach Dunkerque is as a diversion on the homeward leg of a journey from further afield: perhaps, if carless, of a trip around north eastern France such as that described in Chapter 3. For those without cars, there are frequent through trains from Arras (calling at Béthune and Hazebrouck) and several trains (changing at the latter) from Lille, while from Calais there are bus and train services.

Arrival at Dunkerque station is a convenient introduction to the city. The modern glass-fronted building and the square facing it are modest affairs, more in character with a quiet country town than this great industrial metropolis. The bus station is in the same square and there is a sprinkling of hotels and restaurants including among the latter the fairly pricey Richelieu adjoining the rail station.

To see the best of the place it is as well to go about a mile up town from the station. A suitable base in that area is the 3-star Europ Hôtel, some of the room prices being quite low, and amenities on the premises including two well-run restaurants, one specialising in grills and the other in fish dishes.

A few yards from the Europ Hôtel is the embarkation wharf for the sightseeing boats which in 1¼ hours provide a tour of Dunkerque's great showpiece: the harbour and shipyards with good views of a great variety of shipping. Within a few minutes' walk are the city's two most distinguished old buildings, the Town Hall and the church of St Eloi. In addition, the fine modern museum and theatre, the tourist office and the excellent Codec supermarket, with its great circular fruit and vegetable stall, are but a few steps from these sights. In walking around this section of the city centre the visitor will gain a more favourable impression than in the part nearer the rail station as described earlier in this chapter; and although it still cannot be said that Dunkerque is a place of beauty it does become possible to appreciate its workaday way of life and to admire the occasional square or building, park, canal or tree-lined boulevard of interest or distinction.

Just over half a mile from the hotel is the beginning of the Malo seafront and, in dry weather, this is where to go for the evening. On the way, quite near the hotel, is the very adequate restaurant, Victoire; and just off the seafront is the small 2-star hotel, Trianon, a good alternative to the Europ for anyone preferring the quieter life of Malo to the hustle and pressures of central Dunkerque.

Malo has a long, enormously wide, hard sandy beach, as enjoyable as any short of Le Touquet, with the high cranes and gantries of the commercial harbour at one end and endless sand-dune country into Belgium beyond the flats at the other. The pleasantly informal promenade is lined by a varied assortment of houses, small hotels, cafés and restaurants, nearly all of four storeys or less and a few of them survivors from the pre-war age. When we were there, people were arriving in a stream of cars for an evening drink or dinner, joining the strolling residents, many of whom are fortunate to combine a working life in darkest Dunkerque with a home life in the relative eldorado of Malo-les-Bains. Just off the seafront there is a compact network of residential streets, attractive boulevards and squares, good shops and all the amenities of a prosperous small town. There are also a casino, swimming pool and skating rink.

A menu-gazing meander the length of the seafront brought us to Le Pingouin restaurant, close by the casino, with windows offering clear views of the sea and a bill of fare specialising in fish dishes. The arrangement of this restaurant is agreeable, and the food excellent. For 68F we had a first-class *soupe de poissons* followed by *raie au beurre noir* and a good *tarte aux pommes*. When we emerged, night had fallen but the seafront and its cafés and restaurants were still alive.

The immediate French hinterland and neighbouring coastline, a limited area sandwiched between the Belgian frontier and the environs of Calais, is generally flat and divided by dykes with occasional clusters of trees providing windbreaks for farms and houses. A few miles to the east is the small resort of **Bray Dunes**; inland is the charming and skilfully rebuilt small market town of **Bergues**, home of a cheese; and to the west is the small port of **Gravelines** with its Vaubanesque fortifications. By car, this round can be managed easily in three to four hours and, given a little longer, each place may be reached by direct bus or train services from Dunkerque.

After that tour and a lunch-time snack in Malo, we came back into Dunkerque to complete our view of that city and to collect information about local attractions, in particular about opportunities to view the beaches from which the Dunkerque evacuation took place in 1940. To our surprise, we were unable either at the tourist office or at an information desk in the museum to get any definite guidance apart from a display in the museum showing embarkations from Malo-les-Bains and the nearby harbour breakwater. There appeared to be no visit facilities to help tourists to recall this great epic; and so ill-informed was the lady in the tourist office that, when asked which beaches were used for evacuations during World War II, she replied the nearest ones were really rather a long way away: in Normandy! It seems that, with true French logic and realism, the Dunkerque evacuation is dismissed as a disastrous retreat whereas the more sentimental British, with their ability to look on the bright side in moments of catastrophe, prefer to live with the legend that the same event was some kind of British triumph. With so much bread and butter coming their way from British trippers, it might pay the Dunkerque tourist managers to be less chauvinistic.

Information about transport from central Dunkerque to the ferry terminals was also hard to come by. Later, we learned that the best bet for Sally Viking passengers is to gate-crash the returning trippers' buses (in Place Jean Bart) although, clearly, this would not work for the morning departures. However, there is also an occasional public service bus (route 7) from the rail station forecourt, but this provides no official connection with the ferries, Sally Viking or Sealink, and no one could say how close its route comes to the terminal buildings.

Diary Day 2

1655 We cast off from meter berth in Place de la République and, avoiding the now familiar city centre shoals, bowl merrily along the highway, guided by the plentiful 'Car Ferry' signs; and

1710 We join the waiting queues of cars.

1735 The Princess greets us with open bows; and

1810 We sail for England. Ship is again pretty full, including a new (to us) army of day trippers, all cheerfully satiated, being homeward bound, tensions apparent on outward voyages from England having gone overboard. Duty free shop pretty busy, restaurant fairly quiet, the latter possibly because it displays no menu yet seems to expect payment in advance. We find quiet corner and continue work on travel notes.

1930 English time (2030 French time). Ramsgate.

1955 Ashore. Warm, dry, sun about to set. Besides coaches for the organised groups, we hear news of bus into town centre. Busy nearby car park for those who use own car to Ramsgate ferry terminal and then cross on foot. But information about all this so sparse, even in Swedish, that many passengers, some with baggage, still walking their weary way into town.

2000 We head for London; and, after safe passage,

2145 We are home.

Chapter 3 : A Round of Cities

Summary

In this itinerary all travel in France is *by train* along routes with frequent enough services to allow changes of mind at short notice. At each of the seven cities and towns visited, the station is near the centre and, where overnight stops are made, is within 300 metres of one or more suitable hotels.

Day *Itineraries*

1st Early afternoon, arrive **Calais** by hovercraft from Dover. Select hotel, check in. (*Rec*: Meurice, Richelieu.) Snack. (*Rec*: Au Monteur brasserie.) Walkabout Rue Royale area–docks–beach, choose restaurant for dinner. (*Rec*: La Diligence.)

2nd Walkabout Boulevard Jacquard area, visit museums, lunch. (*Rec*: Le Channel.) Mid-afternoon, train to **St Omer** for 2½ hour walkabout. Continue to **Lille.** Check in and seek dinner. (*Rec*: Bellevue, Carlton hotels, then Le Compostelle restaurant, Vega brasserie.)

3rd Walkabout, snack lunch. (*Rec*: station brasserie, any likely café in shopping area.) Mid-afternoon, train to **Arras**, select hotel, check in. (*Rec*: Univers if only the best will do, or adjoining station, Moderne.) Early evening, walkabout and settle for dinner. (*Rec*: Ambassadeur restaurant, Grandes Arcades brasserie.)

4th Early start. Train to **Valenciennes** (changing at Douai), then back to **Douai**, allowing over 2 hours in each for walkabouts, regaining Arras early afternoon. If time permits, snack in Valenciennes (*Rec*: La Paix café, station

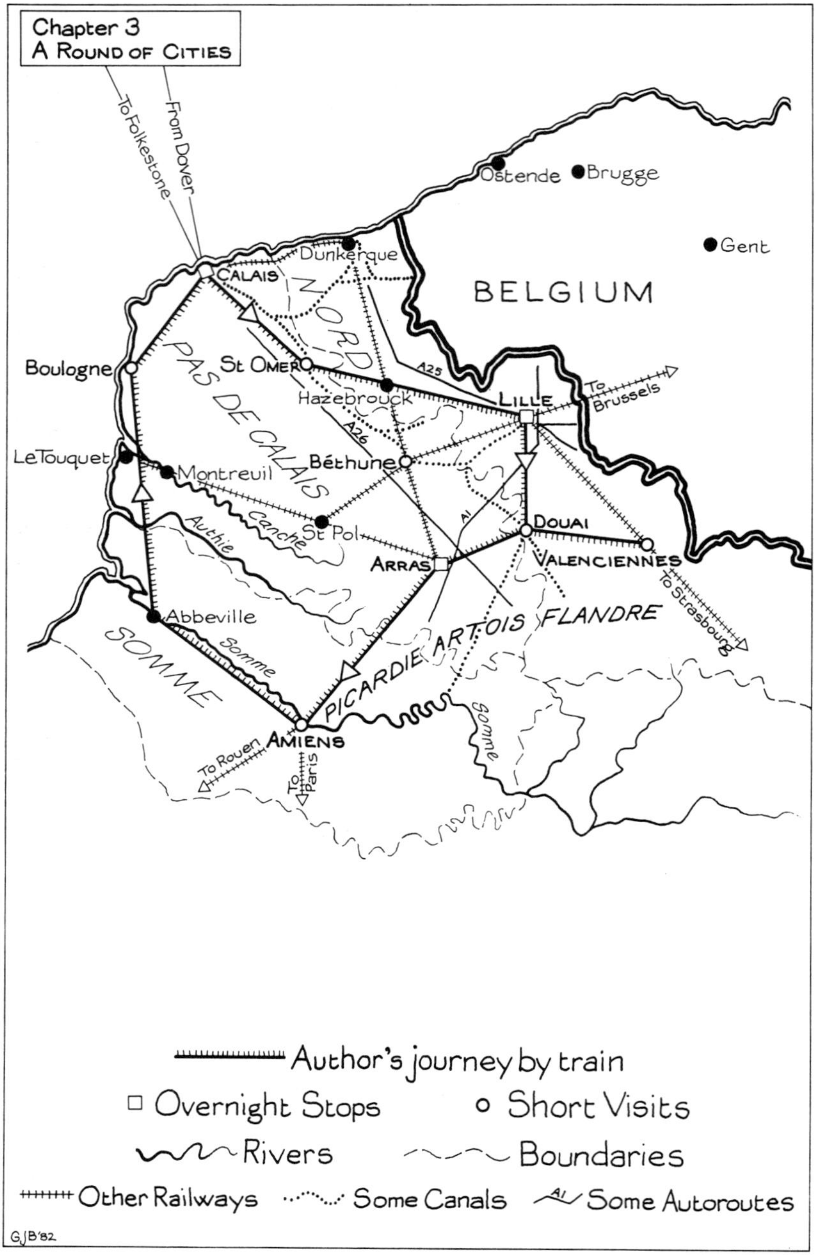
Chapter 3
A Round of Cities
To Folkestone
From Dover
Ostende
Brugge
Gent
Dunkerque
Calais
BELGIUM
NORD
PAS DE CALAIS
St Omer
Boulogne
A25
Hazebrouck
Lille
To Brussels
A26
LeTouquet
Montreuil
Béthune
Canche
Authie
St Pol
A1
Douai
Valenciennes
Arras
To Strasbourg
Abbeville
SOMME
Somme
PICARDIE
ARTOIS
FLANDRE
Amiens
To Rouen
To Paris
Somme
Author's journey by train
Overnight Stops
Short Visits
Rivers
Boundaries
Other Railways
Some Canals
A1
Some Autoroutes
GJB'82

buffet) or Douai (*Rec*: Etna Pizzeria, any likely café in Place d'Armes, station buffet). Conclude Arras walkabout.

5th Train to **Amiens**, arriving early or late morning, for walkabout of 2–6 hours, depending also on forward timing. Snack. (*Rec*: La Tartine.) Leave early or mid-afternoon by fast train via Calais or Boulogne, ferry to Folkestone (or hovercraft to Dover), train to London, arriving early or late evening.

The author's journey in this chapter is contained within 5 days: if more time can be spared, particularly in and around Arras, so much the better. On the other hand, by fitting in Valenciennes and Douai between Lille and Arras and spending a little less time everywhere, the essence of the trip could be condensed quite well into 4 days.

Author's Narrative

The standard leaflet on **Calais** available to tourists has a jolly French sailor on its cover and, under the heading 'A Short Stay in Calais', he enjoins 'Let me be your Guide'. The leaflet's text provides a well set out and efficient introduction to a port through which, as the matelot explains, more British holidaymakers pass each year than any other city or town on the European mainland.

I began my journey to those parts in a motorcoach from Bloomsbury direct to the Dover hoverport, starting from a gloomy little coach station below the Royal National Hotel. Soon after reporting, with others, at a desk in a basement room resembling a dungeon, I took my baggage to the loading bay, waited to see it safely stowed, boarded the coach and settled down for a two-hour non-stop journey across Kent. My companions, mostly young adults, included two with whom I became acquainted: a cheerful lady from Australia researching folklore for a TV programme and a bright-eyed young bride-to-be en route to Paris to meet her lover, an Army officer stationed on the Rhine. Both seemed visibly shaken when I said I would not be going beyond Calais. 'Calais!' they exclaimed. 'Whoever goes to Calais?'

At the Dover hoverport building, an impressive copy of a smart up-to-date airport, we waited our turn to retrieve our baggage from the coach's boot and then stood in line to be checked in once again, after which, having enjoyed two more queues, one for passport control and another at the boarding gate, we were before long being whisked across the Channel, a trifle bumpily, on what Hoverspeed endearingly call 'Flight' 522.

In the shiny, brand new hoverport terminal at Calais we stood in our sixth sheep pen of the day, for the immigration ritual, and in our seventh, to recover baggage, thus attaining a rate of about one queue every half-hour on the three-and-a-half-hour journey, an experience which lessens somewhat the illusion of speed provided by the hovercraft.

A short journey by bus through bleak industrial territory brought me to the Calais Ville station which is undistinguished; and, contrary to the normal rule in France that a station buffet is a good place for a local meal, the bar and buffet at Calais Ville seemed to confine themselves to drinks and snacks in a rather tawdry setting: a pity, because it is a bright room with views into the distance in two directions.

And it is the distance that matters, the station itself being on a windswept mound above the railway tracks, beside featureless expanses of road and canal: to your left, at the approach to the tourist area of the town, you come first upon a terrace or two of modern buildings, one of them housing the tourist office and another, heaven help us, a café called L'Hovercraft; but down to your right, after an unpromising start, there is, at least, Calais' one great splendid building, a massive edifice with soaring tower in the Flemish Renaissance style, the Town Hall.

* * * *

But first we must proceed down the left-hand slope, across the canal and on to the island which forms the original centre of the town, where nowadays virtually all the hotels and a good many of the cafés and restaurants are concentrated. This area is bisected by its main throughfare and shopping street, Rue Royale, which following its original curves, has been pleasantly rebuilt since World War II.

Several charming small parks lie quietly and unexpectedly around the town. One of these, Parc Richelieu, greets you on your right at the approach to Rue Royale and fronting onto it, facing south, is one of the town's more attractive and less expensive hotels, the 2-star Richelieu, run hospitably and with great good nature by the resident owners, who clearly enjoy presiding over their 15-room establishment, the best rooms of which have large windows and balconies overlooking the park. A few yards away, behind Calais' modern and well-presented Musée des Beaux Arts, is the town's best hotel, the 3-star Meurice. This is an old-established though largely rebuilt hotel, well-known over the years to British motorists staying overnight on their way home across the Channel. In its modern wing beside the gardens at the back the rooms are somewhat basic, lacking even a wardrobe or drawers, though each has a well arranged bathroom; but in the older part of the building there are several larger and better appointed bedrooms including some facing south although deprived of any view of the park by the intervening museum. Most of these bedrooms and all the public rooms of the hotel are furnished in period style, giving a nice impression of opulence in a distinctly French idiom. The hotel is well run in a matter-of-fact way and, as now appears to be the custom in hotels of this class, at least in this part of France, you carry your own bags to your room.

This hotel has a connecting door to the next-door restaurant, La Diligence, the most distinguished eating place in Calais and run on formal lines with charm and courtesy by a deftly professional young team. You eat in a panelled room with an

Edwardian-style décor, and for 60F I enjoyed *fricassée* of mushrooms, followed by a *sautée* of veal *aux poivrons* and the house *tarte aux pommes*, the last-named being so elderly that I felt it should have been confined to an old tarts' home long ago. But this was untypical, the other dishes being entirely acceptable, though tending to the bland side.

Calais has numerous cafés, brasseries and restaurants listed fully in a leaflet under the rather grand heading '*Calais: Station Balnéaire et Climatique, 1er Port de Voyageurs de France*'. This leaflet also has a map printed the right way up, that is with north at the top, whereas the leaflet with chatty sailor on its front has the map upside down. At the far end of Rue Royale, past Place d'Armes, just around the corner in Boulevard de la Résistance and facing part of the harbour, is Calais' best all-round restaurant, Le Channel, with seating in comfortable high-backed chairs, in a wood-panelled room. For the price of 52F, I enjoyed lobster mousse, chicken sautéed in wine sauce and apple tart, this time a tart of a more nubile consistency. Favoured as much by the French as by the tourist, it has a cheerful atmosphere and is particularly good with seafood, the aroma greeting you as you enter, a nice touch being the king prawns served with your aperitif.

At the cheaper end of the scale, among the more run-of-the-mill brasseries, I had a very adequate and briskly served omelette at Au Monteur, sitting in the window with a good view of all the activity in Place d'Armes, a rather tatty square contained by squat buildings, all somewhat reminiscent of a Sudanese market place. At the far end is the large supermarket Gro, the most accessible to visitors on foot and, accordingly, a little more expensive than its competitors further afield while, by the near end, is the Maison du Fromage, the ideal if not the cheapest place for your cheese shopping.

Between the Rue Royale area and the sea lie the main harbour and commercial areas of the town, including the Sealink and Townsend Thoresen ferry terminals, the Gare Maritime railhead, cargo handling wharves and a spacious yacht marina; and beyond that, over to the left, clear of the industrial area but backed by grim-looking high-rise flats, is the wide and sandy beach stretching away past Blériot Plage and Blanc Nez towards Cap Gris Nez. Overlooking this beach are three restaurants side by side of which the most expensive and most recommended is the spacious Côte d'Argent. With its fine sea views and despite its position, which in winter appears to be somewhat isolated, this is an all-the-year round target for local people as well as the occasional tourist.

*   *   *   *

So much for those parts of Calais best known to the passing holidaymaker. On your second day, if you walk around beyond the beaten track you will come upon several surprises, the more pleasant for being unexpected. Two or three blocks from the Rue Royale are several residential areas with quiet, well laid-out streets and local shopping neighbourhoods, not least the houses with their gardens, and the low-rise apartment blocks fronting the avenue which gives access to the moated citadelle, all providing a tranquil refuge from the rush of life.

Most surprising, however, is the extensive area which is seldom penetrated by the hurrying visitor: the area down to the right, past the Town Hall, when you emerge from Calais Ville station. This, the townfolks' own main shopping and business district, stretches along and beyond Boulevard Jacquard, a handsome street in the best French provincial-city style about the same length (and effectively a southward continuation of) Rue Royale. The Boulevard Jacquard district is good for clothes shopping, including the wares of popular department stores as well as boutiques. It has two supermarkets, Centre Commercial and Prix Gros, and close by is a concentration of the lace factories for which Calais has long been famous.

In the early 19th century lace-making craftsmen from Nottingham, in search of better prospects, crossed the Channel to set up their businesses in Calais, and several of the companies still carry English names and use English terminology. One factory may nowadays be shared by several concerns, the tall, sometimes derelict looking buildings often arranged around a modest central courtyard. But appearances may be deceptive: inside, there is likely to be modern equipment worked by busy employees who are usually pleased to find the time to welcome anyone who knocks on the door and asks to be shown round. Most of the lace produced in Calais is exported, but fluctuations in fashion and competition have made the market increasingly unstable; and Calais which has long since diversified its industries, retains its lace-making traditions on grounds of sentiment and prestige rather than for compelling economic reasons.

* * * *

My last port of call was the remarkable War Museum housed in a former German bunker in Parc St Pierre, facing the Town Hall and Rodin's justly famous bronze statue of the heroic Burghers of Calais who, in 1347, gave themselves up to the wrath of Edward III in order to save their city. The exhibits, comprising a medley of photographs, newspaper cuttings, descriptive material, small models and bits of equipment (almost like a family album of souvenirs) provide a grim reminder, the more poignant for the way the simple material tells its dreadful story with such quiet dignity, of the oppressive German occupation and destruction of this hardy seaport following the retreat of the British forces in that area in 1940. And just as the Burghers of Calais were ready to be sacrificed to save the honour of the town and the lives of their fellow citizens in the 14th century, so in World War II, as the price for harbouring and supporting British soldiers, leading Calais citizens lost their lives or their liberty at the hands of an enemy for whom, as this museum shows, little love was lost.

The history of Calais over many centuries has been to an exceptional extent inextricably tied up with England and, indeed, for over 200 years, following Edward III's famous siege in 1347, Calais was part of England. Two queens feature most prominently in the story of the English occupation of this seaport: it was Edward's wife, Philippa, who pleaded successfully with her husband for the lives of the six brave Burghers; and when the port was returned to the French, Mary Tudor was so stricken that she lamented bitterly, 'When I am dead and opened you shall find Calais lying in my heart.' In later centuries Calais became the first foreign foothold for peripatetic English tourists, with regular crossings from 1819, and today Calais is pleased to claim that in the summer season a car ferry or hovercraft leaves England for that port every 20 minutes.

Certainly, the people of Calais extend remarkably warm hospitality towards the constant stream of British visitors. And it is, indeed, its affable, sturdy people who make Calais what it is. The town may be short of outstanding sights and scenery but it is a cheerful place, and the longer you stay in it the more it grows on you.

* * * *

From the War Museum to Calais Ville station is but a few steps, and in mid-afternoon I boarded a train for Lille. In the hinterland of Calais there are a number of important and often attractive cities and smaller towns, many of which have features of interest to the discerning tourist. The largest of these and, indeed, the third largest city in France, heart of an extensive heavy industrial, engineering, textile and commercial area, is Lille, a little over an hour by train from Calais. Arras, capital of Artois, and Amiens, capital of Picardy are also within easy reach by train.

An important virtue of this area to the visitor who chooses to travel without his car is the convenience and density of the railway network serving its towns and cities. Of these, in this chapter, besides Calais, Lille, Arras and Amiens, we will be visiting by train St Omer, Valenciennes and Douai, taking note also of Béthune, in each case leading hotels and restaurants as well as principal sights and other amenities for visitors being mostly within a few minutes' walk of the railway station. And, as I aim to show, given some advance planning with the help of a suitable timetable such as the *Thomas Cook Continental Timetable*, it is possible within a five-day trip from London to visit all these places and, at the same time, gain an impression of the varied countryside, including industrial landscapes and former battlefields, in which they are set.

Half an hour after leaving Calais, the Lille train reaches the magnificent station of **St Omer.** Before continuing to Lille, it is possible to spend two to three hours in St Omer, a distinguished small town with a handsome, lofty cathedral surrounded by cobbled streets of 18th- and 19th-century houses. The sleepy, peaceful atmosphere may be somewhat spoiled by speakers attached to buildings which blare forth rather tuneless pop music. There are several pedestrianised shopping streets around the Town Hall, while the leading hotel is 2-star Bretagne, barely five minutes' walk from the station, with a Michelin-rosette restaurant. Other recommended restaurants include Le Cygne and La Truye qui File, but the best value for money may be obtained even closer to the station at the smaller, more modest Chez Henriette.

St Omer, sometimes with affectionate exaggeration but some truth called the 'Venice of the North', is a main stop on a canal system which is more extensive in this corner of France than may generally be realised. The Neuffoise canal splits temporarily here into two, one part by-passing the town and the other cutting through it near the station forecourt. To the north, at Watten, this canal divides again into three sections: one for Calais, another for Gravelines and the third for Dunkerque. To the south, at Aire, the canal has an indirect branch to Lille; and further on, beyond Béthune, it divides two ways, one section for Lille and the other for Douai. After Douai, there are yet three more divisions: one for Arras, one for Valenciennes, the third down the Somme for Amiens and, eventually, once again, the English Channel. Thus, *in theory*, given time, patience and perseverance, much of the travel described in this chapter could be attempted by water or, at least, by combinations of train and barge or pleasure boat.

Then, between St Omer and Watten, flanking and straddling both the railway and the canal, is the remarkable, little-known network of small lakes and waterways, described altogether as **Le Marais Audomarois** and in part as **Les Watergangs.** Unspoiled and indeed largely unapproachable by road, this is wonderfully tranquil country for fishing, boating or walking. Its main raison d'être, however, has long been market gardening, particularly of cauliflowers. The gardens are worked mainly as smallholdings from canal-girt cottages, many of them linked with each other and the world at large only by boat or by footpaths and small, humped bridges.

The whole of this lovely survival from a pre-atomic era is soon to have park status. The present administration, based in St Omer, has the delightfully explicit title of 'Syndicat Mixte Pour la Mise en Valeur Touristique des Marais de l'Audomarois'; and the tourist office of St Omer can help with leaflets and information about the various facilities: walking, fishing permits, boat hire, guided tours and the availability of gîtes and camp sites.

*　　*　　*　　*

And so, after this pleasant interlude, on (by train) to **Lille.** I hope when you visit that city they will have finished digging up the place to build their metro, a process which, for some time, has been causing such disarray in the city centre that Lille's amorphous station must be one of the few of its kind in France in which one has no wish to linger. Having negotiated the various holes in the ground and the noise and clatter of the earth-moving machinery, you emerge into a congested and mildly confusing muddle of bus stops, traffic, pedestrian crossings and cafes spilling on to narrow pavements. On leaving the station keep going straight ahead and in only 300 yards you will reach the relative haven of Place du Théâtre, heart of this great city. Hereabouts are most of the leading hotels, none higher than 3-star, and all geared more to the everyday needs of businessmen than to the whims of tourists. The best of this group is the Bellevue although I also have pleasant memories of the Mapotel Carlton.

Right next door to this hotel is an amusing open plan complex of shops, café and restaurant on three floors, the Vega Store. The vivid green and yellow décor, broken by metallic bannisters and railings, with high glass partitions, wide windows and attractive tiled floors, is reminiscent of some of the bolder 1930s designs. The amenities on the ground floor include, besides the café, a book shop, record shop and hairdresser; and one pleasant feature of the restaurant upstairs is the good view of the life of the city through its windows. If you like to see a view while you eat or drink, a facility usually associated with France, then make the most of the Vega as, surprisingly, many restaurants and cafés in Lille seem almost as curtained off and introspective as an English pub.

One of the most highly recommended is Le Compostelle in Rue St Etienne, describing itself enthusiastically as a *'relais flamand du 16ième siècle'*. My dinner there for 80F comprised a remarkable *terrine de trois poissons à sauce d'oseille*, followed by *estouffade de boeuf provençale* and, a speciality of the house, *gâteau aux noix*. I was lucky to get away with this price as, at the first attempt, the waiter handed me a bill of fare which offered only a menu at 120F, but I was unlucky when, at the end of the meal, I allowed a Calvados to be served, without prior consultation, out of a cobwebby, rather pretentious bottle at the price of 40F plus service. My chief memory of that restaurant is its location in a lifeless basement with a phony cellar-like décor, all part of an ultra-modern and far from 16th century building; and slightly slapdash service by a team from whom one would expect a higher degree of professionalism. But the *gâteau aux noix* was excellent.

* * * *

For the tourist of serious intent, the locals recommend walks around what remains of the old quarter. This part of Lille is in a state of decay and even the cathedral is in poor condition. The forlorn atmosphere kept recurring in other parts of the city, which was clearly in the grip of the European trade recession, the textile industries so important in this region being particularly hard hit: with more than 40,000 out of work in the Lille–Roubaix–Tourcoing area alone, an increase of some 34% over the previous year, an air of gloom is, perhaps, hardly surprising.

Even so, Lille did not strike me as a city that has ever achieved anything like *joie de vivre.* Before starting these journeys I had written, in French, to the chambers of commerce and tourist authorities in all the major cities across northern France explaining what I was about and Lille was one of the very few which not only failed to acknowledge but which, according to the French Tourist Office in London, seemed incapable of supplying even them with tourist literature.

One good feature is the central area of pedestrianised streets lined with expensive shops, and there is also a fairly opulent looking business quarter in and around Avenue Foch. The gardens there display statues not only of General de Gaulle, who was born in Lille, but also of Rousseau, who must be equally revered by the Lillois even if nobody in the smart café opposite could tell me why.

In general Lille is a dour city, but many fine buildings and handsome streets are to be found in and near the centre, including its redeeming feature, the Musée des Beaux Arts, housed in a magnificent 19th-century building and one of the few surviving glories of greater and more prosperous days. There are paintings from many of the important schools, Dutch, Flemish and French, including Impressionist artists, being notably well represented. The city is worth a visit if only to admire these great works and for the wandering tourist, particularly if travelling by train, Lille's position at the hub of a regional network makes it a convenient base.

* * * *

In the afternoon of the third day I made tracks for **Arras**, a half-hour train ride from Lille. First impressions of Arras are stimulating. This city, capital of Artois, is a sociable and animated town with good shopping, good eating, enough culture and several impressive relics of the past. In the station square are various hotels of which the 3-star Moderne, facing three ways, with some rooms having balconies and a brasserie at street level, is recommended. The best hotel in Arras, the 3-star Univers, a former monastery, is ten minutes' walk from the station up Rue Gambetta, a pleasant if traffic filled street of former town houses.

The Univers has great charm, fine reception rooms and a rather grand atmosphere, although, on close scrutiny, is a little past its best. The management is competent but does make the visitor feel he is one in rather a long line of transient guests and the apparent peace of the courtyard, around which the hotel is built, is a bit of a delusion since it serves to echo and magnify the shouts of children and the barking of dogs.

Among the notable features of this interesting city is the surprisingly vast Grande Place, enclosed by long stretches of arcaded 16th- and 17th-century Flemish buildings, which except on market days seems to have been frozen in time. A handful of restaurants hide behind the columns in this elegant but verdureless square, and plenty goes on below it in the form of a large underground car park; I found pleasure in the convivial Grandes Arcades brasserie-restaurant, where I enjoyed a jolly meal for 56F, the highlight of which was an outstanding *poulet sauté à l'estragon*.

Among other important survivals are Place des Héros,

dominated by a magnificent City Hall, a splendid example of 17th-century Flemish Renaissance architecture, with a 250-foot belfry. The Abbaye St-Vaast, founded in the 7th century, now houses the museum and art gallery, including the marvellous collection of tapestries for which the town has long been famous. The city hall and abbey were badly damaged during World War I when Arras, which was very close to the front line, suffered repeated attacks, but both have been remarkably well restored. In another quarter of town, on the way to the Citadelle, the octagonal but seemingly circular Place Victor Hugo, a gem of a small enclosed 'square', is also worth a look, as is the citadelle itself, built by the ubiquitous Vauban and now a barracks situated in a quiet park. I hesitate to include the cathedral among the desirable sights as it is of comparatively recent origin, rather tucked away in a corner and, except in size, not very impressive, and, like too many other historic buildings in this part of France, it is becoming dilapidated, on the brink of seeming unloved.

As some of the streets curve and disappear round bends, it is not always easy to get your bearings in Arras but it offers unexpected short-cuts for pedestrians, hidden corners, pretty vistas and always a selection of old buildings on which to feast the eye, many with carved wooden doors and delicate stucco work of floral designs. Indeed, there are numerous reminders of the city's prosperous and creative past, with its long history of grain, cloth and wool trading. Today, there may be ugly industrial development on the outskirts but the city centre has largely retained its charm, and while Arras was the birthplace in 1758 of the infamous lawyer Robespierre, contemporary members of his profession appear finally to have achieved respectability judging by the smart name plates outside several of the grandest-looking houses.

Arras has many inviting shops, cafés and restaurants. Rue Ronville, in particular, caters for the rich and elegant, with most of the top designers being represented in Sergine K, while the main street, Rue Ernestale, also contains a number of shops of note, including an excellent leather goods retailer, Au Cuir de France, and the mouth-watering patisserie, Paulo Boulangerie. As for the eating places, there are enough cafés, tea rooms, brasseries and restaurants to keep a hungry gourmand happy for three or four days, most notable among these being the Ambassadeur, with its Michelin rosette, which stands right beside the railway station.

* * * *

Within a few miles of this city, mostly to the north, on either side of the A26 highway, there are many British war cemeteries, filled with the victims of World War I, as well as other 'memorials', such as trenches and dug-outs. There is also the famous memorial on Vimy Ridge bearing the names of 64,000 Canadians while, nearby, at France's Lorette memorial, a large lantern is kept alight in memory of many thousands of known and unknown French soldiers who died there. These cemeteries are mostly tended lovingly by gardeners, often descendants of those buried there, who are a mine of information on the history of the war; and the War Graves Commission, which has its office just outside the city, can supply less colourful although possibly more accurate data. Unfortunately, it is virtually impossible to visit the cemeteries without a car since there is no public transport and organised tours are infrequent, but a map and photographs are contained in a leaflet called 'La Route du Souvenir' issued by a regional tourist office, L'Union Départmentale des Offices de Tourisme Syndicats d'Initiative du Pas-de-Calais, based in St Omer.

From Arras, in little more than a single morning, I made a trip by train to Valenciennes and Douai, the latter being a stop, usually involving a change of trains, on the way to the former (and each, incidentally, having its own direct rail link with Lille).

Of the two, **Douai** is the larger and, in historic terms, the more significant, having once been the home of the Flanders Parliament, though its 'capital' status today has been reduced somewhat to that of headquarters of France's Northern Coal Board.

Douai has been largely rebuilt after being much damaged during the two World Wars. My first destination was the Musée, housed in the old Charterhouse dating from the 16th century, and situated between two canals towards the north-western corner of the city. This attractive building, in a peaceful residential area, houses a surprisingly rich collection of paintings, although, sadly, not all of them were adequately lit, but the curator was anxious to help and seemed genuinely pleased to welcome visitors.

I then set forth on foot to discover parts of the old city. The tourist leaflet depicts a Venice-like scene of gracious buildings beside a canal, but be warned: these are at least half-an-hour's walk away and not really in the town centre. To reach them I threaded my way through tranquil streets to the banks of the Scarpe, along which I walked for some distance, admiring blossom-filled gardens and colourful window boxes. Douai was a university city until 1887, when its faculties were transferred to Lille, and many fine buildings survive in this quarter, where a studious atmosphere lingers.

This mood is quickly dispelled, however, nearer the centre of what is now, essentially, an industrial town. Here the narrow pavements are crowded with shoppers and the streets with small cars and motorbikes, but the Belfry, made famous both by Victor Hugo's description and by Corot in a painting that now hangs in the Louvre, should be seen. Close by, in Place d'Armes, tables and chairs were being put outside the cafés, although the spring weather was certainly no better than it would have been in England. Here you will find the recommended restaurant, La Terrasse, and the pleasant Etna Pizzeria. On the way back to the station I passed a bustling market in Place Carnot, and in the station itself I found a homely buffet under the cheerful supervision of a friendly Madame who made it seem that, to serve the Englishman with a *citron pressé*, was one of life's great pleasures.

* * * *

While Douai today is chatty, exuberant and provincial, **Valenciennes**, although smaller, has a surprisingly cosmopolitan stance and self-assurance. The buildings seem larger, the streets wider, the squares grander, the people more at ease.

Once again, almost all the good hotels and restaurants are right beside the station. The best hotels are the 3-star Mapotel Grand, which looked distinctly inviting, and the 2-star Bristol, while the best-value restaurants are the Buffet-Gare with its Michelin rosette; La Dodenne, just alongside; and La Coupole, a first-floor brasserie opposite the station.

If you can tear yourself away from the gastronomic corner, you will find the Musée des Beaux Arts housed in an elegant, mansion-style building on the far side of the central area. In a manufacturing city known sometimes both as the 'Athens of the North' and as a *'cité intellectuelle'* the museum is an important focus and contains some interesting paintings and sculptures, including those of several Valenciennes-born men who gained international reputations. On my way back I passed through the lovely Place d'Armes, the heart and meeting place of the community, a refuge in the centre of the shopping area, with ample space to walk around, and several pavement cafés, La Paix being the most attractive. This square is dominated by the splendidly ornate façade of the Town Hall, but do not look too far: behind the magnificent front is a featureles modern glass building which, although cleverly hidden, is a regrettable contradiction.

Valenciennes, in the words of its glossy brochure *'Une Ville pour Ses Habitants'*, is rather like its Town Hall: a concoction of new and old, of earthy and urbane; and it is the people, as much as their buildings, who set its style. Valenciennes intrigued me and, given more time, I should like to go again.

*　*　*　*

On the fifth and final day, after two nights in Arras, I took a morning train to **Amiens** and, within the hour, was emerging out of yet another imposing railway building into one of the biggest station squares of all, dominated by an incongruous high tower, the work of Perret, creator of modern Le Havre. Only five minutes' walk away, in breathtaking contrast, stands the pride of Amiens, a cathedral of outstanding splendour, set beautifully in a square close by the River Somme and perhaps the most impressive large-scale survival in the whole of this war-torn corner of northern France. It was built originally in the 13th century and the side chapels were added between 1292 and 1376. The right tower was built in the 14th but destroyed during the 15th century; whilst the transept spire was rebuilt after being burned down in 1528. Apart from the marvellous scale and unity of its proportions you will enjoy the exterior statuary and the interior carvings, which in number and in detail are quite remarkable.

Apart from the cathedral, however, it is difficult to find anything in Amiens which is arrestingly spectacular: some 60% of it was destroyed during the two World Wars, and it has been largely rebuilt. One small, stone building of note is the delightful and largely unsung circus in Place Longueville. And this is no obsolescent relic: when I looked inquisitively round the door I was, to my pleasure, greeted by the sight of performing animals rehearsing for that night's show. The Musée de Picardie deserves a visit for its fine collection of paintings and sculptures; and it is also worth making the short walk beside the Somme to the Hortillonages, another complex of market gardens laced with tiny canals akin to but much less extensive than those adjoining St Omer.

Amiens is a spacious and rather sedate city with quite good shops scattered around the central area including a useful department store, Nouvelles Galeries, off Place Gambetta. Close by is the tourist office, one of the more obliging of its species, the offerings of which include a helpful guide to walks around Amiens. If you want to stay the night and only the best will do, choose the 3-star Hôtel Univers on the main street 300 yards from the station. With one side facing a quiet square, this is an old-style, fairly smart provincial-city hotel in the best French tradition. For meals the station buffet is not really up to scratch but, near the cathedral, La Tartine offers good value. With its gastronomic heritage of superb vegetables, confectionery and such delicacies as *pâté de canard en croûte*, good food is never far away. And for evening entertainment, besides the circus, there are the puppets or *cabotans*, unique to Amiens, which depict scenes from the city's history.

* * * *

After a morning's trudge around Amiens I must have clocked up at least 30 miles of sightseeing on foot along hard pavements since landing at Calais and was ready for home. Besides, station platforms in France are a long way below carriage-floor level and my finer memories were tending to be overlaid by those of yet another climb, more often than not with suitcase and guide-book-laden briefcase, into yet another train and then, at the next stop, by yet another walk into unfamiliar streets, ever hopeful eyes alert for noteworthy happenings.

I had one more port of call in mind, either as a side trip from Arras, or en route to the coast from or via that city, but a furious corn was saying 'No'. And so I missed **Béthune** which, by all accounts, is well worth mentioning in the same breath as St Omer, Valenciennes and Douai. For a small town of barely 30,000 inhabitants Béthune has an unusual range of facilities: a university, two theatres, a museum, art gallery, religious buildings, sports complexes, a large swimming pool and on its very fine main square, Grande Place, the inevitable belfry in its tall tower. This one, dating from the 14th century, presides over a network of caves and underground galleries which are thought to have been the workshops of weavers of various textiles of years gone by, theirs being an important traditional industry in this district.

There are several hotels and restaurants and Béthune, painstakingly restored in Flemish tradition after the devastation in World War I, on the boundary between agricultural and mining areas, is well placed on the road as well as the railway systems.

* * * *

From Amiens on any summer day, between about midday and early evening, there are at least seven fast-train departures for Calais or Boulogne, connecting at one or other of these ports with ferries or hovercraft, with further connections at Folkestone or Dover, giving arrivals by train at Victoria or Charing Cross between tea time and late evening. I chose the early afternoon boat train for Calais Maritime and boarded the third coach from the front, ensuring arrival opposite the platform exit, from which it is but a few yards to the gangway giving access to the waiting Sealink ferry.

The crossing time to Folkestone is a little over 1½ hours. On arrival at the Harbour station, having negotiated the covered way, a gauntlet of eager porters masking a cluster of available baggage trolleys, passport control (the *only* queue, all the way) and the green side of the custom hall, I found the connecting train to Victoria ready to receive us. And here, once again, take note: if you are in a hurry to get away at Victoria join the rear of the train at Folkestone Harbour for, when it reaches the top of the incline, the train reverses its direction, thus ensuring that the first shall, indeed, be last. QED, but only through learning the hard way; and now the secret is out, no doubt they will change the system.

I have arrived often at Victoria and it provides a more reassuring welcome to the great metropolis of London than the dingy basement from which, a few days earlier, I had begun my odyssey. And it is well endowed with telephone booths, a useful feature for anyone anxious to make an early appointment with his chiropodist.

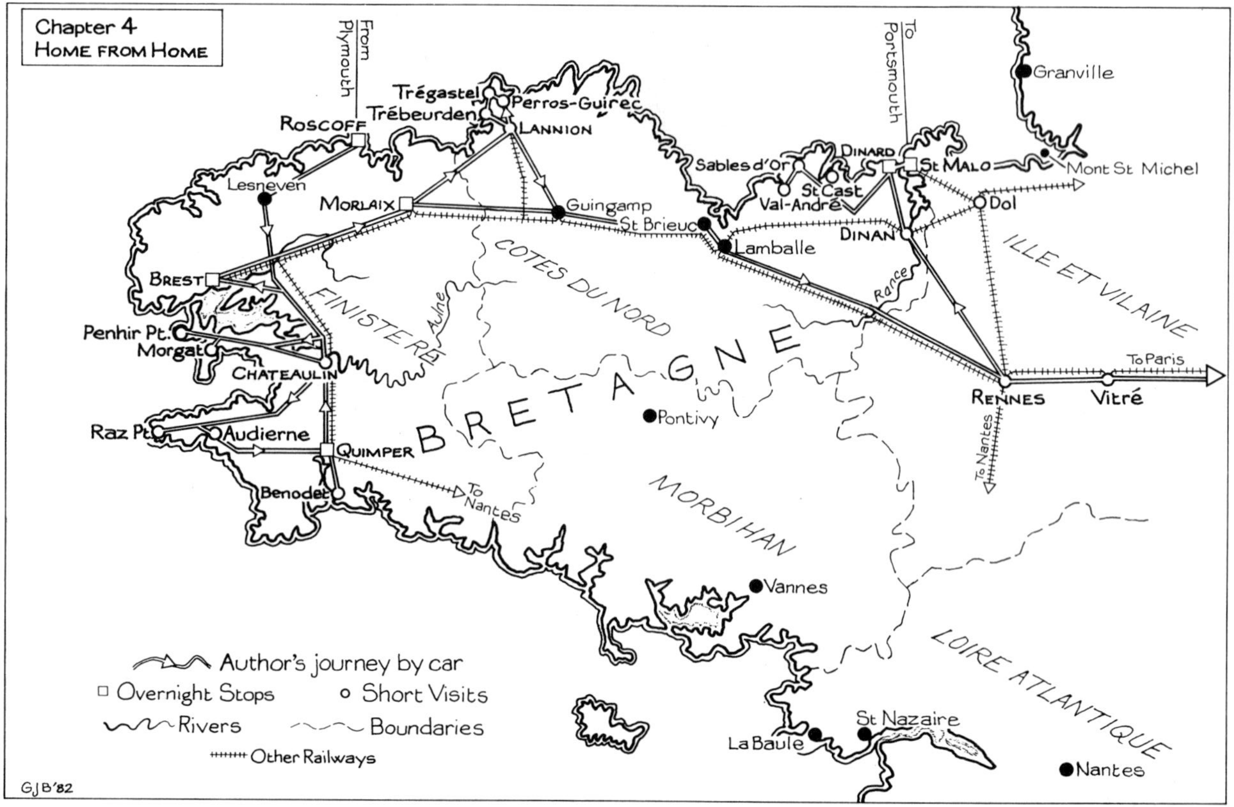

Chapter 4
HOME FROM HOME
From Plymouth
To Portsmouth
Granville
Trégastel
Perros-Guirec
Trébeurden
LANNION
ROSCOFF
Sables d'Or
DINARD
St MALO
Mont St Michel
Lesneven
St Cast
Val-André
MORLAIX
Guingamp
St Brieuc
Dol
DINAN
Lamballe
BREST
ILLE ET VILAINE
COTES DU NORD
Rance
FINISTERE
Aulne
Penhir Pt.
Morgat
CHATEAULIN
To Paris
RENNES
Vitré
BRETAGNE
Pontivy
Raz Pt.
Audierne
QUIMPER
To Nantes
Benodet
To Nantes
MORBIHAN
Vannes
LOIRE ATLANTIQUE
Author's journey by car
Overnight Stops
Short Visits
Rivers
Boundaries
Other Railways
St Nazaire
La Baule
Nantes
GJB'82

Chapter 4 : Home from Home

Summary

The following sums up a journey by car along the northern Brittany littoral and its hinterland which is feasible within the Brittany Ferries 5-day tourer return, arriving at Roscoff and leaving from St Malo :

Day	*With Car*
1st	Midday, leave Plymouth for **Roscoff** arriving late evening. Stay overnight. (*Rec*: Le Triton, des Bains.)
2nd	After 3-hour walkabout, proceed by shortest route (D788, D770, N165, D791), by-passing Brest, to **Crozon Peninsula**; visit Penhir Point and Morgat; divert inland (D887) to **Châteaulin**; and continue by fast road (N165) to **Brest** arriving early evening. Tour city, select hotel, check in. (*Rec*: Voyageurs, Vauban.) Walkabout, choose restaurant for dinner. (*Rec*: restaurant or brasserie in Voyageurs, the station restaurant.)
3rd	Explore Brest in morning, then take fast road (N12) to **Morlaix.** Select hotel, check in. (*Rec*: Europe.) Walkabout, dinner. (*Rec*: Le Coquin, brasserie in hotel, cafés around Place des Otages.)
4th	Early start. Leave Morlaix for **Pink Granite Coast** (D786), calling briefly at Perros-Guirec, Trébeurden and Lannion. Continue to **Rennes** (D767, N12), arriving mid afternoon. Tour city, select hotel, check in. (*Rec*: Du Guesclin, Cheval d'Or, Voyageurs.) Walkabout, choose restaurant for dinner. (*Rec*: station restaurant, choice of brasseries in station square, Corsaire in old quarter.)

5th Explore Rennes until mid morning. Side trip to **Vitré** if time permits (N157). On to **Dinan** (N137, D27) to arrive early afternoon for 1–2 hour walkabout. Thence to **Dinard** (D766) arriving early evening. Select hotel, check in. (*Rec*: Reine Hortense if in funds, otherwise Printania with sea view, des Bains without.) Walkabout, dinner. (*Rec*: restaurants in Grand or Printania hotels, brasseries around Place République.)

6th Early start. By car or on foot, sample the local coastline. Then final walk in Dinard before continuing to **St Malo**, arriving early afternoon after brief tour of its environs. Walkabout St Malo and in the evening choose restaurant for dinner. (*Rec*: Duchesse Anne, Pomme d'Or, brasseries around Place Chateaubriand, Thermes on Paramé beach: if staying overnight, consider France-Chateaubriand or Noguette hotels.) After dinner, board ferry for overnight passage to Portsmouth.

By adding a couple of days to this journey in the form of a diversion between Châteaulin and Brest it is possible to sample the nearest section of Brittany's south coast. By eliminating Crozon Peninsula and Brest from the given itinerary, the same diversion could be managed without extra time, Morlaix then becoming the next stop after Benodet. In the latter case, if time were of the essence, the schedule could be :

2nd After 3-hour walkabout (in Roscoff) proceed by fastest route to **Châteaulin** for short visit. Then continue (D107) via Douarnenez to **Raz Peninsula**, calling at Audierne and Raz Point itself. Return eastward (D784) to **Quimper**, arriving in the early evening. Select hotel, check in, walkabout, dinner. (Ample choice, no special recommendations.)

3rd Early start. After final walkabout in Quimper, go south

(D34) to **Benodet** and nearby coast for brief visit. Thence back through Quimper and cross-country (D785) to arrive mid afternoon in **Morlaix**. (Then, as in main itinerary above.)

Without Car

A traveller could quite easily cover the main features of the foregoing itineraries mainly by train, partly by bus and boat, in 6–9 days, though the sequence of places and some overnight stops would be slightly different and parts of the remoter coastlines are not readily accessible by public transport. It is important to note however, that while the others are located conveniently, the rail stations at Roscoff and St Malo are quite a step from their respective town centres and ferry terminals (though the latter station has a bus service into both St Malo and Dinard). Moreover, in Morlaix it is a very steep climb up to the railway. Thus, briefly :

Day	*Without Car*
1st	Plymouth – **Roscoff** by ferry. Stay overnight.
2nd	Early afternoon, Roscoff – **Morlaix** by train. Break journey about 3 hours and on by train to arrive **Brest** for dinner. Stay 1 or 2 nights.
3rd	If 2 nights, side trip by boat across Brest harbour and for part tour of **Crozon Peninsula** by connecting bus, regaining Brest late afternoon.
4th	Late morning, Brest – **Quimper** by train. Overnight in Quimper, including possible side trip to **Benodet** by local bus.
5th	Quimper – **Châteaulin** by train in morning. Break journey about 3 hours and on by train changing at Brest and Plouaret, to arrive **Lannion** early evening. Stay overnight; consider side trip by local bus to **Perros-Guirec.** (Alter-

natively, remain in train at Plouaret to arrive Rennes early evening.)

6th Leave Lannion late morning by train via Plouaret to arrive **Rennes** mid afternoon. Stay overnight. (Alternatively, if Rennes was reached the previous evening, use part of this day for side trip by train to **Vitré**).

7th Leave Rennes mid morning by train, changing at Dol, to arrive **Dinan** late morning. After 2 hours in Dinan, return by train to Dol, changing there, to arrive **St Malo** mid afternoon or, if available, take boat from Dinan down river to St Malo arriving early evening. (Alternatively, remain in first train at Dol to arrive St Malo at lunch time, and from there later side trip to Dinan by train via Dol, or by direct bus and/or boat.) Stay 1–2 nights in St Malo.

8th Side trip by local ferry to **Dinard.** Explore this resort and nearby coastline on foot, returning to St Malo by bus or ferry. Embark that night for England or

9th Leave St Malo by ferry, either late morning by day service or late evening by overnight service, to Portsmouth.

Author's Narrative

Brittany has long been a favourite destination for the British holidaymaker not wanting to go too far from home; for families with children and for the staider elders; and for people seeking somewhere not too unfamiliar with amenities which, they hope, are neither too expensive nor sophisticated. On the map and in the guide books, Brittany seems reassuring: its scenery and fishing ports have a look of Cornwall and, like that county, it is off the beaten track, has a splendid coast and has a Celtic population. So, the British expect to feel at home there; and in my view, certainly, Brittany does seem less foreign, less truly French than the other areas of northern France covered by this book.

I was sailing with Brittany Ferries from Plymouth to Roscoff, traditionally a route where vegetables get priority. But my ship, the *Cornouailles*, was clean, comfortable and well run by an efficient, good humoured crew. Admittedly, we sailed an hour late, but by this time the restaurant, An Triskell, was offering in a pleasant ambience, tables for two as well as four, a four-course meal of good standard for 65F comprising *hors d'oeuvres*, choice of *boeuf bourguignonne* or *poulet rôti* or *côte de porc rôti*, followed by cheese and dessert, with a quarter bottle of wine thrown in for good measure. Even the cafeteria was dishing out a tempting chicken stew, though its opening hours were rather short, and towards the end of its stint the choice of food was minimal. But the bar seemed to be available most of the time.

But the hold was very crowded, particularly by lorries and the worst feature was the lengthy loading and unloading process. This ship, among others, with stern loading only has to get every vehicle turned around in a very congested hold for disembarkation, with the heaviest often boarded last and given pride of place. In my experience, from the time of embarkation to the time when I was able to drive my own car ashore amounted to nearly nine hours and, this being a day crossing, a ridiculous waste of holiday time; and it was 2130 French time before I reached my Roscoff hotel.

*   *   *   *

Roscoff was a very pleasant surprise, a close-knit agricultural and trading town, a seaside resort and a port, commercial, fishing and *de plaisance*, the whole with the cheerful air of a busy and successful small community. Most of the buildings fronting the winding streets and the wide esplanade are in a warm, grey stone and nearly all, modern as well as ancient, in keeping with their environment; and all over the town behind high stone walls or thick hedges, there are small fields thick with growing vegetables. In the evening, the mood of the town is leisurely, though its many small hotels and bars and the transient ferry-borne population give it a certain vitality.

My overnight hotel, the 2-star Le Triton, was not on the water front but made up for this by its excellent facilities and the ready hospitality of Madame, who seemed always to be at her place behind the desk whenever any guest required attention; but with a next-door farmer out at dawn among his vegetables, accompanied by tractor, barking dog and children, she could have had no problem with oversleeping guests. In the centre of Roscoff, overlooking the water, are three attractive 1-star hotels, des Bains, Arcades and Talabardon, of which the first is perhaps the best. About half a mile towards the ferry port is Roscoff's leading hotel, the 3-star Brittany, and from here there is a superb view, over the fishing port, of the town clustered around its church tower. This opulent hotel has spacious public rooms, but the piped music permeating the reception area was not encouraging and a swimming pool in its back garden was disappointingly sited.

Roscoff is a place to linger in and, with a car, makes an ideal centre for the adjacent coastlines with their wide, sandy bays broken by savage rocky outcrops. However, the hinterland is rather flat and boring as I discovered on the day after my arrival when I was to cross it by the shortest route, through Plesneven, a pleasant inland market town, to the other side of Brest. I was bound for the **Crozon Peninsula** where, according to the *Michelin Green Guide*, 'nowhere else (in Brittany) do the sea and coast reach such heights of grim beauty with the giddy steepness of the cliffs, the colouring of the rocks and the fury of the sea breaking on the reefs'. In addition, some of the small towns and seaside villages on this peninsula have considerable charm and there are some very fine hard-sand beaches, although south-facing **Morgat,** despite the warm sun which was bathing it, seemed rather a sad place, and the town of Crozon which gives its name to the peninsula was unremarkable.

*　　*　　*　　*

The best discovery I was to make in this locality, a few kilometres east of the isthmus, on the River Aulne, served by the Brest-Quimper railway and close to the Brest-Quimper highway, was **Châteaulin**, a delightful small town lining the curving banks of its famous salmon river, with a handsome, waterside tree-lined boulevard and a happy arrangement of shops, houses and public buildings: a very agreeable place in which to spend an hour or two. A mile along the road towards Brest, facing open countryside across the same river near its highest tidal point and accessible to deep-water yachts, stands the 2-star Au Bon Accueil, an inviting country hostelry with a restaurant popular with French families as well as visitors for both its fare and its view. Whether by car or by train Châteaulin makes a good base from which to explore this part of west Brittany, the immediate countryside being more undulating, woodier and prettier than the norm in these inland parts. One advantage of being car-borne is that you can put up conveniently at Au Bon Accueil.

* * * *

Châteaulin is a convenient point of departure for the western end of Brittany's south coast and a diversion may be made either as an addition to my main journey or, if time is limited, in lieu of my visits to Crozon Peninsula and Brest. In any case a diversion southward, besides adding interest to the itinerary, has two advantages: this accessible coastline, lying well to the south of the latitude of Paris, has a climate as good as that on any of the more distant coasts of France and Spain facing the Bay of Biscay; and so far as the region covered by this book is concerned, this end of southern Brittany is the warmest bet for alfresco holidays and for rural self-catering holidays of all kinds.

For the present purpose I confine my diversion to the sunnier side of **Raz Peninsula** and to the coastline down-river from Quimper, including the attractive south-facing resorts of Audierne and Benodet, both within 120 kilometres of Roscoff. I should like to take you further afield but the geography of

Brittany is such that as you go eastward along its south coast to the Loire the distances from both Roscoff and St Malo lengthen quite sharply, putting many attractive resorts, from Concarneau to La Baule, beyond my present brief.

However, Audierne and Benodet in conjunction with Quimper are a fair sample, and I have had a good report of a Brittany Ferries gîte holiday in Benodet. The gîte was built of granite, with pine panelling and floors, fully equipped with the necessary comforts of modern living, and spotlessly clean. The gîtes in this area, purpose-built, are out in the country and, while produce from local farms is sometimes available on the doorstep, a car is usually necessary to fetch and carry from the local shops and markets.

Benodet, a delightful small estuary town, is set in a well wooded countryside which provides a contrast with and escape from the tidal waters and seaside which, for most tourists, are the main *raison d'être* of a district with good sands and fine coastal scenery. The best local beaches include one from Ile Tudy to Pointe de Combrit and one from Pointe de Mousterlin to Beg Meil, each about 5 kilometres long and both of gleaming white sand. Boat trips are available along the coast and up the Odet to Quimper. The terrain also invites walking, and it is good country for picnics, beach games, crab-hunting and the like. This is ideal holiday country for families with young children.

Quimper, wet or fine, makes an admirable centre. The cathedral, the hillside gardens overlooking the river, the markets indoor and outdoor, the art gallery, the variety of eating places and the busy good humour of the people all add to Quimper's attractions.

The Raz Promontory, the tip of the peninsula, is spectacular, not unlike Lands End, with marvellous views inland as well as seaward. Apart from attractive but north-facing **Douarnenez**, through which the approach to this corner of the world is made from Châteaulin, **Audierne**, with its large harbour in a pleasant setting, and extensive neighbouring beaches, there does not seem to be much of exceptional interest on Raz Peninsula; and, stuck out into the Atlantic, it is wilder and wetter than the more sheltered Quimper-Benodet axis.

*   *   *   *

Our next port of call was **Brest**, a city said to be the wettest in France, specially prone to deluges of rain interspersed with thick mists swirling into the roadstead from the ocean. And this is how it was on my first day. One of the few features recommended in the guide books is a viewing platform on a raised escarpment overlooking the vast expanse of harbour. From it you expect to see the land and islands (including Crozon Peninsula) which encircle the approaches to this historic naval port and are linked, in some cases, by direct boat services with Brest. Alas for this much vaunted feature, I could see nothing from the platform except the modern, expanding commercial docks just below, and one or two grey warship shapes in the enveloping drizzle. No wonder one of Brest's most popular shops is Au Parapluie Brisé, the entire stock of which is a practical and, evidently, timely assortment of umbrellas.

The best value hotel is the 3-star Voyageurs in Avenue Georges Clemenceau. This has a useful range of rooms from quite inexpensive singles without private facilities to attractive doubles looking on to the adjoining park. And it boasts Brest's only Michelin-rosette restaurant, a luxurious first-floor amenity with fine views through wide windows. The set menu, a little pricey at 128F, comprised four courses, my own quite satisfying choice being *langoustines* with an excellent mayonnaise, followed by cuts of salmon served hot with a caper sauce, then *filet mignon porcelets* with a lightly flavoured mushroom and pepper sauce, and in conclusion a pleasant *tarte aux pommes*. On the ground floor there is also a simple and more popular brasserie which offered an acceptable menu for 42F. Altogether the Voyageurs is a very welcome refuge on a wet Brest day.

If you want a less expensive hotel try the 2-star Vauban next door; and if you wish to eat fairly cheaply and quite well have a go at the first-floor restaurant by the railway station. This has broad views across the harbour and a very adequate menu in a friendly atmosphere for around 62F, including moules in a butter sauce, *coq au vin* and cheese or dessert.

As French cities go, I found rather a dearth of inviting bars and cafés, and not much chance of a seat from which to view the passing scene. As for shopping, the traffic-congested and people-crowded Rue Jean Jaurès is the local Oxford Street, the indoor facilities here being supplemented by market-type stalls on the pavements and in the square at the down-town end of the street. A southward extension, Rue de Siam, is more relaxed and has fewer shops but most of these are of better quality: particularly worth visiting around the corner in Rue de Lyon is an exceptional leather goods establishment, the Quinou Maroquinerie. But be warned: into some of these streets, recorded music and spoken advertisements blare forth from loudspeakers on the sides of the buildings.

* * * *

The morning after my arrival dawned bright and sunny and the town revealed itself as a not unpleasant arrangement of wide streets, squares and parks. To me, the best sight within the city was the gorge of the River Penfeld, containing the winding linear naval dockyard, which can be seen from several vantage points on the promenade beside Boulevard Jean Moulin, to the north of the splendid castle. Here also was an agreeable district flanked by middle-class flats, their view along the gorge being reminiscent of Valetta, all this within a stone's throw of the heart of the city. And nearby, among the trees, quietly standing sentinel above the harbour was a surprising find: a high column in a starkly modern style commemorating the words 'Erected by the United States of America to commemorate the achievements of the Naval Forces of the United States and France during the World War'. After a search, MCMXVIII in small letters revealed which war. So: and what, I wondered, was there about the endeavours of these two navies in the First World War to justify this particular salute; and why did the Americans choose to make their quite grand gesture in such an inconspicuous corner of France?

I made tracks from Brest towards Morlaix by the Brest-Rennes-Paris expressway. I broke the journey at **St Thegonnec** to sample one of Brittany's best known parish closes. Here, behind the village church, was a small enclosure with a chapel, some tomb stones and an array of statuaries, as well as a shop offering tourist literature and guided tours. The village itself, which happened to be *en fête*, provided an agreeable interlude, a fair and a bowls tournament attracting animated attention in a large open space close to the church.

Morlaix, only a few miles inland from Roscoff, is a delight, a snug and picturesque small town contained in a steep gorge at the head of an estuary, the whole in the shadow of a soaring double viaduct which carries the main Brest-Rennes-Paris railway across the valley. This is a very fine example of railway architecture but means that the local people have a pretty stiff climb up to their station. The congested centre of this town, of which its leading hotel, the 2-star Europe, is an attractive feature, carries too much car traffic for comfort, and in this narrowest section of the gorge the effect is slightly claustrophobic, but the network of streets broadens as you go seaward along Place des Otages and under the viaduct. Here flanked by ascending rows of buildings is a pleasant area, including a yacht harbour, with room to wander and an interesting choice of shops and cafés. A good meal may be enjoyed in Le Coquin restaurant, with the Europe's brasserie, the hub of local business life, as a satisfactory alternative. For shoppers Morlaix boasts one of the largest hypermarkets in France.

From Morlaix it is but a step to the **Pink Granite Coast**, for which I set off early next morning, the gateway from this direction being the neat compact riverside town of **Lannion** with its tidy, pedestrianised shopping alleyways reminiscent of St Malo and its choice selection of old buildings. Close by is the leading resort of this coastline, **Perros-Guirec**, with its dramatic rocky outcrops and sandy beaches; along with other places at the west end of this coast such as **Trégastel** with its separated beaches and wild coastline astride a north-facing promontory, and **Trébeurden** in its beautiful south-facing setting with panoramic views of the Breton coastline towards Roscoff, this proved a disappointment.

*   *   *   *

Rennes is a very large city divided into two distinct halves, almost as though it was two different places. The relatively modern quarter, of which the railway and bus stations are focal points, contains most of the hotels and numerous eating places. Whenever I visit this city it seems to be bulging at the seams with conference goers and tourists: on an earlier visit the only way I could get horizontal for the night was by buying myself a couchette on the Paris overnight express. Montparnasse station at dawn has its points but is hardly the ideal starting place for a Rennes walkabout.

On this occasion several of the 2-star and 1-star hotels were full, but that hotel of character and distinction, the 3-star du Guesclin, took pity on me. I had to pay more than I had intended, but my spacious room, with a balcony and windows in two directions, gave me much pleasure.

The more usual attractions for visitors are in the older quarter on the north side of the River Vilaine, a mile or so from the railway station. Here is an attractive assortment of cobbled streets with a number of ancient buildings containing some of Rennes' smarter shops and restaurants and, rather hidden away in their midst, a cathedral, originally of the 6th-century but, after being burned down and rebuilt, now largely 19th-century. The classier restaurants in these dark and narrow streets, some of them in rather pretentious 'olde worlde' guise, did not appeal to me though, of those I investigated, I did take quite a fancy to the Corsaire. Simpler and more cheerful meals can be obtained in a number of inexpensive brasseries in and near the large square facing the railway station and this is a pleasant and, certainly, the liveliest part of Rennes to eat or drink in.

On the dividing line between the two halves of the city is its distinguished museum and art gallery and adjoining the northern section, towards the university, is the Jardin du Thabor. This park, of which a former garden of the nearby Benedictine Abbey forms part, is a pleasant place in which to stroll. It covers over 25 acres and contains a botanical garden, formal French and rose gardens, some unusual rhododendrons and azaleas, lawns, trees, a wooded area with caves and a stream running down a gorge, zoo pens and an aviary.

The essence of Rennes is, I think, well hidden from the tourist. This great provincial capital is, with quiet pride, a leading cultural, scientific and manufacturing centre concerned as much with evolving forms as with established tastes and practices; and I sense that the locals feel themselves a cut above their business and holiday visitors. Travel broadens the mind but only if other minds emerge to grapple with; and Rennes bears out my long-held view that tourism, and not least conference going, mainly broadens the bottom.

*   *   *   *

Vitré is some 40 kilometres from Rennes and, if time allows, is well worth a diversion. As every guide book agrees, Vitré is a prime Breton example of a really well preserved, historic town. It is built on raised ground, and dominated by its fairy-tale castle, one side of which overlooks the River Vilaine while the other commands a valley containing the railway on which Vitré is a stop between Rennes and Paris. Striking views may be gained on approach along the Brest Road and from a suggested viewing table, the Tertres Noires.

There are two main squares, one of them in front of the castle, and both flanked by fine old buildings. The hilly Rue Beaudrairie is a very attractive old street with its cobbles and medieval, half-timbered slate-roofed houses, beautifully preserved, the atmosphere here being surprisingly light and airy. The castle itself, now half in ruins, has several towers and turrets, while the Notre Dame, although rather dark inside, has some beautiful stained glass windows and an interesting outside pulpit. There is a fine promenade which follows the old base of the ramparts.

* * * *

In the early afternoon of this, my fifth day in France, I came upon **Dinan** standing squarely against the skyline, long impregnable behind its high ramparts. After crossing the River Rance the ascending road, skirting the great wall, wound its way into the city where, in Place du Guesclin, I found ample room to park.

Dinan, another gem of conservation, is essentially an 'atmosphere' town, one which on a short visit invites absorbed perambulation and general appraisal of the old streets, buildings and fortifications rather than a detailed study of the individual attractions. The tourist office offers a map outlining a recommended route and drawing attention to the main sites in the old town, including the Basilica St Sauveur and other religious buildings, the Jardin Anglais, the sweeping panorama from Promenade des Petites Fosses, including views down the lovely Rance estuary, and various items of interest in the narrow medieval streets centred mainly on Rue de l'Horloge and Place des Cordeliers. Dinan also makes a feature of the products of local craftsmen whose workshops are open to visitors and whose work is on sale in a cluster of shops gathered around Rue de Jeruzal. The output includes jewellery as well as pottery and glassware. The 2-star Marguerite will take good care of you if you decide to stay overnight in this enchanting town.

I made my visit by car but, as I point out in my Summary of the present chapter, Dinan offers an ideal destination for a day-trip from Dinard to St Malo by boat, by bus, or by connecting trains, changing at Dol, or by combinations of these means. If you go by train you have the advantage of a glimpse of Dinan station, which has a striking Art Deco interior, with a colourful ceiling depicting towns and landmarks of the Ille et Vilaine and, if you wish, between one train and the next, of Dol-de-Bretagne.

A visit to **Dol-de-Bretagne** makes a pleasant break, the shopping area being in a well preserved medieval district with a maze of narrow streets, on the edge of which stands the surprisingly large, sturdily built cathedral dating from the 13th century. A brisk circuit of the town may be completed within an hour including a walk along the shady Promenade des Douves on the ramparts, from which there are views of the countryside, and if you tire of all that and, perhaps, miss your connection you can enjoy an easygoing spell of train spotting at Dol station, a junction on the local network of secondary and branch lines, with trains to St Brieuc (via Dinan), St Malo, Cherbourg and Rennes. At least two dozen trains converge daily on this sleepy backwater.

*   *   *   *

The approach to Dinard from landward is unexciting. There is a neat, compact airport with a pleasant upstairs brasserie and restaurant just outside the town which, as it envelops you, offers an air of well-groomed and neatly-trimmed *comme-il-faut* security; and it was a relief to arrive there after my fairly arduous trek across northern Brittany from Brest down to Rennes and northward again, via Vitré and Dinan, on this final lap.

Dinard, 'gem' of the **Emerald Coast**, is a well-bred, once highly fashionable resort, set prettily on a lush ridge between estuary and open sea, the villa-studded promontories separated by small bays and promenades, natural hub of a network of more or less level coastal footpaths, ideal for walking. From these, as you make your way westward around a series of headlands and across unsuspected beaches set into small bays, there is an ever-changing view of sea, coastline and rocky outcrops, with the splendid walled city of St Malo reappearing all the time like a mirage in one direction and Cap Fréhel elusively and distantly in the other. On a sunny afternoon, the vivid green streaks of sea explain why this is named, aptly, the Emerald Coast.

A quite frequent bus service runs parallel to this section of coastline (to Lancreux or St Briac) and can take you back to Dinard when you have walked enough: there are stops just inland of most bays. To explore the Emerald Coast further on you will need your yacht, failing which a car will do. I particularly liked St Cast, facing towards Dinard, and just beyond Fréhel, Sables d'Or and Val André.

The fairly extensive sand beach at **St Cast** has, at one end, the 3-star Ar Vro hotel, a quietly dignified and secluded mansion in its own grounds and, at the other, the rather jollier 2-star Etoile de Mer, the restaurant of which has good views over the port and along the beach. **Sables d'Or** consists of a short, broad thoroughfare in an unspoilt setting behind a wide, undeveloped beach flanked by pine trees: a restful and picturesque oasis between stretches of relatively bleak and sometimes dramatic coastline. And here, by the thoroughfare, are some inviting hotels, notably the quite palatial Ajoncs d'Or and its simpler neighbour, the Voile d'Or. At **Val André**, an attractive small resort set in a fine bay, with long-distance views along the neighbouring Pink Granite Coast, the sea front is traffic-free. By the port, is the Cotriade Michelin-rosette restaurant, while just behind it is the pleasant 2-star Hôtel des Bains with its sociable town-centre café/brasserie. The tourist office here was particularly obliging, not least in explaining and evaluating some of the excellent local walks.

* * * *

Dinard itself offers its own compact arrangement of mostly sandy beaches, an Olympic-size swimming pool, a casino, an extensive tennis club, an acceptable golf course, a yacht marina and a range of other sports and entertainments. It is a fairly staid resort with endearing reminders of its genteel hey-day, and its laconic mood and the smiling good temper of its people give it a special welcoming quality.

Just behind this beach, Plage de L'Ecluse, with private access to it, and with a lovely view of St Malo over the nearest Dinard headland, is an elegant survival, the 4-star, south-east facing Villa-Hôtel Reine Hortense, arguably the most distinguished hotel in northern Brittany. With only ten bedrooms and managed with professional aplomb and a personal touch by the resident owner, the ambience is that of what it once was, a royal villa, but that creepy take-care-as-someone-is-watching-us feeling sometimes associated with small de-luxe owner-run hotels is well avoided, the sense of freedom assisted by the spaciousness of the rooms, bed and public, and of the garden setting above the beach; and with no restaurant on the premises, you do not have to be constantly praising the cooking.

The other 4-star hotel, the Grand, is also centrally placed, though overlooking the estuary rather than the sea. Below it on a slope down to the river are some impressive gardens which at night, in season, are illuminated in a rather romantic way and become the setting for a *son-et-lumière* with a gentle background of music, the styles of which vary with the day of the week: operetta, jazz and so on. It sounds awful but is done in excellent taste, an aid to nostalgia and to honeymooners, not that there is too much of the latter going on in the Grand these days.

This spacious hotel, very well appointed in 'traditional' style, is now on the motor coach circuit when not in the conference business and otherwise, except in high season, is not all that busy. Between the two rear wings of the hotel, next door to the tennis club, is a perfect enclosed-garden site for a swimming pool, an amenity which would surely be good for trade, the more so as very few hotels in northern France can offer anything comparable. Not that all the clients would take to it: when I called at the Grand the motor coaches in the forecourt were

British, their occupants elderly, and in the bar the radio was serving up the BBC news in English. But the food and service were surprisingly good once the staff had overcome their shock at the sight of an individual cash customer; and the restaurant is an impressive room with good views above the *son-et-lumière* to the more distant lands of dreams bathed that night, inevitably, and one hopes invariably, in shimmering moonlight.

At less expensive levels Dinard offers a wide choice of hotels including the 2-star Printania which rises almost sheer out of the water, Italian style, and has public rooms with dramatic views and a strange, eccentric mixture of Breton and South Sea Island ornaments and decorations. This is a large hotel, well able to absorb coach parties, and although on a busy day there is a touch of the sausage machine, it is well run, the best rooms in the main building are acceptable, the food is palatable: even so, when I put my toe in it must have been just one of those evenings for both the white wine and the mineral water were warm and the service was erratically panic stricken.

The 3-star Crystal, a large, unlovely modern building beside the Reine Hortense, with balconies overlooking the beach, is part hotel and part short-let, self-catering furnished flats. Among the hotels near but not quite by the sea are the cheerful, family-run des Bains and the more austere des Dunes, both 2-star. Cheap eating may be enjoyed in the bars and brasseries behind the casino and around Place de la République.

* * * *

With their distinctive styles, character and attractions Dinard and St Malo, taken together, make an ideal holiday destination. And unless you want to explore the remoter reaches of hinterland and coastline, you can put away your car for the duration. St Malo may be reached from Dinard in a few minutes by bus, calling en route at St Malo station, or by passenger ferry, the latter affording enjoyable views on passage across the estuary of both places, their harbours and the River Rance.

St Malo is a substantial, handsome and historic walled city, rising dramatically out of the sea. Badly damaged in the war, it has been reconstructed with careful adherence to the original and, as the stone weathers, only an experienced eye can tell at medium distance which parts of this city are not in their original condition. The whole fascinating walled area, the Intra Muros, can be viewed from a promenade along the top of the ramparts. And from this pedestrian walkway, besides glimpses up the streets to the centre of the city, you will observe fine, ever-changing views of the sea, the adjacent coastlines, and interesting, although less beautiful, the extensive docks and industrial districts occupying the immediate hinterland of the city.

When you tire of wandering in and around this absorbing city and seek some refreshment you will find a large number of often cheek-by-jowl bistros, brasseries and restaurants, most of them with no outlook beyond the narrow street in which they have their being. In and near the main square, Place Châteaubriand, is a good choice, though for those who wish to spend more I would recommend the Michelin-rosetted Duchesse Anne. Of all the rest the nearby Pomme d'Or is perhaps the most distinguished, at least in style and décor. There are several bars and brasseries in the main square, all pretty busy, and of them, perhaps, the Paris is best.

The highest class hotel, the 3-star Central, is a little cramped and gloomy. I preferred the rambling, old-fashioned, casually run 2-star France-Chateaubriand, with its balconied rooms, some of which face south over the lively square and others (but only from the second floor up, above rampart level) north across the open sea. I was attracted, also, by the small, more intimate 1-star Noguette in a quiet, bright corner in the heart of the city, with an inviting restaurant and high windows overlooking picturesque streets in two directions.

Traditionally a tough, hard-working community, St Malo has long given itself up, without loss of the distinctive character and vitality of its people, to the role of host to the seemingly endless tourist throngs. But if Intra Muros does become too stifling, and strolls along the quaysides pall, go out into the fresh air, beyond the casino, to the wide open spaces of Paramé beach. Here, in the cool of the evening, stride along the hard, white sand, enjoy a satisfying meal in the pleasant if rather suave seaside restaurant of the Thermes Hotel, and then, at sunset, go down again to the beach. As the light fades, watch the changing hues and colours on the ramparts, roofs and cathedral spire of this unique city until, at length, the whole becomes lost in silhouette against the darkening sky.

And thus ended my tour of Brittany: an aperitif in Place Chateaubriand, an enjoyable dinner by Paramé Beach and, in the last afterglow of sunset, straight on board the overnight ferry for Portsmouth.

Chapter 5 : Sea and River

Summary

The journey in this chapter is by car, entering and leaving France through Dieppe, with a fairly straightforward itinerary taking in Rouen and parts of the Seine valley and Alabaster Coast, including Dieppe itself and its environs.

Day	*Itineraries*
1st	Mid morning, leave Newhaven for **Dieppe** arriving mid afternoon. Select hotel, check in. (*Rec*: Univers, Aguado, Select.) Walkabout, dinner. (*Rec*: Univers, Arcades, Armorique, Petite Auberge.)
2nd	Early start. Leave Dieppe for **Etretat** (D925, D940) calling en route at **Fécamp.** After short visit proceed to **Caudebec** (D39, D139, D910, D173, D982) arriving mid afternoon. Select hotel here or at nearby **Villequier**, check in, choose restaurant for dinner, walkabout. (*Rec*: Hotels: Marine, Normandie in Caudebec; Domaine de Villequier, France in Villequier. Restaurants: Normandie, or as good but more expensive, Marine and Domaine.)
3rd	After breakfast continue along Seine valley to **Rouen** (D982) calling en route at **Jumièges**. Tour city, lunch, then walkabout until evening. After early dinner (*Rec*: Château d'O, Pascaline, Havre), take fast road (N27) to Dieppe and stay overnight.
4th	Before embarking at lunch time for Newhaven, tour Dieppe environs, calling at **Varengeville** and **Miromesnil**, with final walkabout in Dieppe; and arrive Newhaven by early evening.

If an extra day can be spared, remain in Rouen overnight (*Rec*:

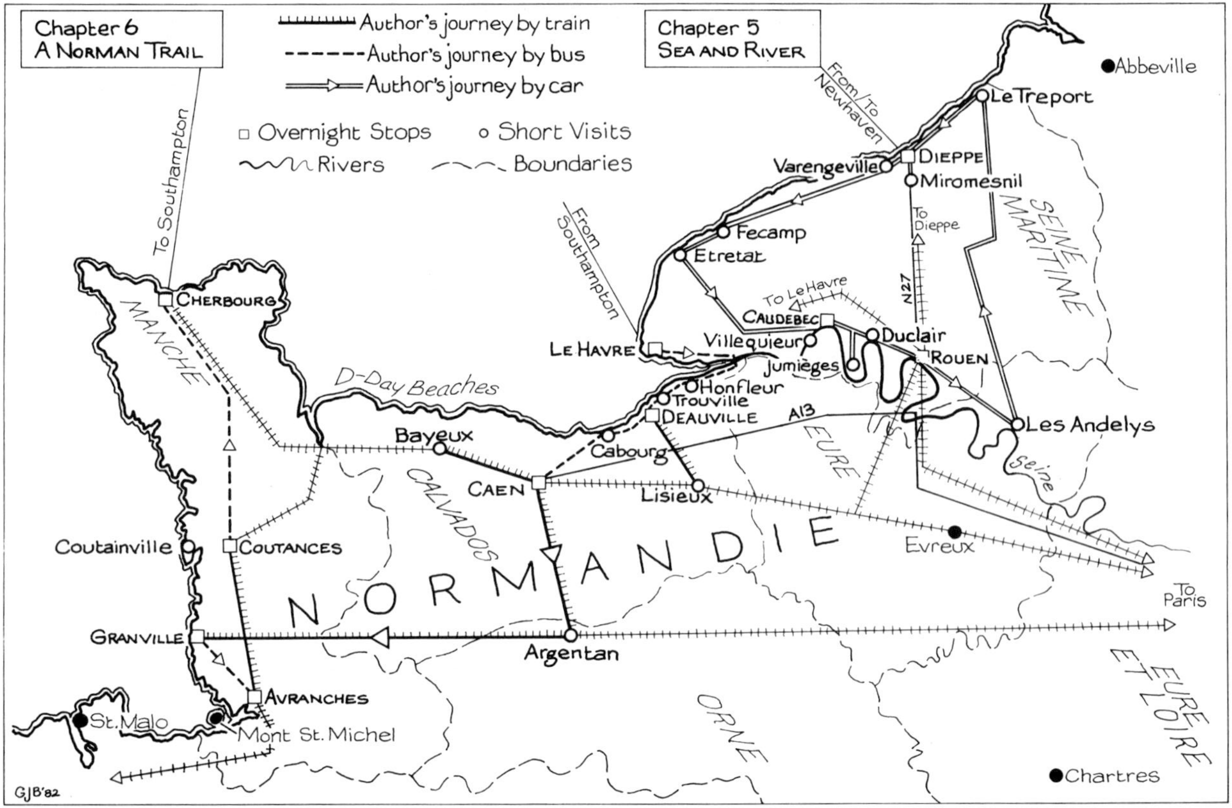
Chapter 6
A Norman Trail
Author's journey by train
Author's journey by bus
Author's journey by car
Overnight Stops
Short Visits
Rivers
Boundaries
Chapter 5
Sea and River
To Southampton
From/To Newhaven
From Southampton
Abbeville
Le Treport
Dieppe
Varengeville
Miromesnil
To Dieppe
Fecamp
Etretat
Seine Maritime
N27
To Le Havre
Caudebec
Duclair
Villequieur
Le Havre
Rouen
Jumièges
Honfleur
Trouville
Deauville
A13
Les Andelys
Cherbourg
Manche
D-Day Beaches
Bayeux
Cabourg
Eure
Seine
Caen
Lisieux
Calvados
Normandie
Evreux
Coutainville
Coutances
To Paris
Granville
Argentan
Avranches
St. Malo
Mont St. Michel
Orne
Eure et Loire
Chartres
GJB'82

Dieppe, Astrid) and, on Day 4, go up river to **Les Andelys** before returning to Dieppe by leisurely cross-country roads, with a possible side trip to **Le Tréport**; and, on Day 5, continue homeward after a morning in and around Dieppe, as shown for Day 4 above. In either case the journey will be completed well within the validity of a Sealink 5-day excursion return.

Author's Narrative

Arrival by ship in **Dieppe** is an exhilarating experience. After leaving the open sea, your vessel winds its way up the ever-narrowing harbour. The enveloping buildings, higher than the ship's mast and almost close enough to touch, with their shops and cafés at ground level, line the quay sides which are themselves busy streets and part of the town centre; and the ship berths so close to Dieppe's high street, Grande Rue, so near the passing cars and pedestrians that legend has it that a short-sighted traffic warden has more than once slapped a parking ticket across its bows. Clever engineering has, however, managed to insert between ferry and the nearest yellow lines an inconspicuous terminal building straddling a pair of railway tracks, and connecting trains from and to Paris and Rouen, worked slowly through the Dieppe streets to the ferry berth, connect with some of the sailings to and from Newhaven. If you are not going on by train you just walk down the terminal steps and, if you like, right into the front seat of a pavement café.

Dieppe has long been my own favourite of the ferry ports on the French side of the Channel and there you are, straight off the ship, close to everything you want. Up to your right is the spacious esplanade and along it, facing the sea, most of the hotels, with the casino at the far end dwarfed by the castle on its high ground commanding the seaward approaches to the harbour. Ahead of you is Grande Rue, the main shopping street, most of it banned to vehicles, the scene on Saturday mornings of one of northern France's most extensive and animated open-air markets. Whether or not you want to buy, this market with its stalls in front of the shops, lining both sides of the street, provides an enjoyable promenade. Everyone is there, the locals in force, the tourists out-numbered, all strolling in procession, rather like an evening *paseo* in Spain.

And then soon after mid-day, suddenly, it is over. The trucks and vans move in, the stalls come down and with the unsold produce empty crates are quickly loaded, and the vendors are gone. The shops prepare to close for their lunch break and, as the strollers drift into the cafés or disappear about their business, the dust carts take briskly over, the refuse collectors making short shrift of all the debris; and there, within half-an-hour, the street, spruce and clean, is cheerfully back to normal.

* * * *

The deft management of this weekly event is one sign that you are in a well run town. Dieppe, host to ever-changing yet seldom obtrusive crowds of tourists, more than two thirds of them British and in former years home of a substantial British colony of artists, writers and high society families visited sometimes by royalty, has contrived to remain true to its own extrovertly French way of life: confident, affable in a plain-speaking way, lively, hospitable, industrious. And Dieppe is not merely a resort and ferry port: its near 30,000 people, whose housing now spreads up and over the adjoining hills, are engaged also in fishing, cargo handling and light industry, their enterprising outlook being well represented by Dieppe's Director of Tourism, Monsieur Agodi, who went out of his way not only to enlighten and entertain me but to ensure that, while I was in his domain, I overlooked none of its numerous attractions.

Besides the casino and the castle-museum with its fine views along the sea front, the compact shopping area and the arcaded buildings by the port, these include the broad esplanade by the shingle beach, backed by a wide grass common offering a sense of space even on a crowded day; and inconspicuously sited, a large outdoor swimming pool and several tennis courts, with their associated cafés, all open to the eyes of any passing spectator. And, as background, the terraces of buildings, mostly quite new, in varies styles, achieve a pleasant harmony.

Adjoining the casino is Dieppe's leading hotel, the modern 4-star Présidence, with its smart roof restaurant and, reputedly, the most sophisticated bar in town. Nearby are the 3-star Univers, with its elegant antique furniture and high gastronomic reputation, and next door the 2-star Windsor with its first-floor restaurant overlooking the sea. Among those without restaurants my own preferences would be the 3-star Aguado, close to the ferry quay and with bedrooms offering views either of the sea or the harbour, and the 2-star Select in a square a few yards inland from the casino, a very good and well run hotel with charm and character.

Eating out, I recall an exceptional meal at the Armorique restaurant on a first floor beside the ferry terminal. This, like most others in Dieppe, specialises in sea food, a mouth-watering display of which awaits the customer just inside the door. Here, for once eating *à la carte*, I enjoyed an outstanding fish soup, *sole à l'estragon* and a bowl of wild strawberries with cream, all this with generous helpings, wine, coffee and first-class service, for not much above 100F. I had another memorable quayside meal in the Arcades restaurant and, although rather cramped but a good deal cheaper, the Petite Auberge bistro can also be recommended. There is an almost endless number of small eating places in the port area and choice can be difficult but, on busy days, do not spend too long menu-gazing: by 12.20 on a summer Sunday there was hardly a spare seat to be found.

Among the several places of interest immediately outside Dieppe are the exquisite Château **Miromesnil**, home of the Count of Vogüé, a beautifully proportioned small castle in a wooded setting. It has both walled and formal gardens and interesting contents including souvenirs of Guy de Maupassant, born there in 1850. A little to the west of Dieppe I found a rather grim but eloquent war museum featuring the ill-fated British-Canadian raid on Dieppe in 1942; and beyond that the enchanting and rather surprising English-style gardens in the Parc des Moutiers in **Varengeville** surrounding a sumptuous turreted mansion rebuilt by Lutyens at an early stage of his career.

*   *   *

Early on day 2 of the present itinerary, with some of the attractions of Dieppe and its environs still in the future, we set off westward along the coast for Etretat, with a brief glimpse of Fécamp on the way. **Fécamp**, once a picturesque haunt of artists and still, primarily, a fishing port, is becoming unattractively commercialised, with a rather bleak beach area and too much expansion, particularly in the form of ugly modern blocks scarring some of the surrounding hill tops. The main square with its pleasant buildings is spoiled by heavy through traffic and an unusual lack of cafés and restaurants, and not even Fécamp's ancient abbey and long association with Benedictine liqueur tempted me to linger in this town.

Etretat in its gorgeous setting between high cliffs is more rewarding. There is a good beach and a number of bright and sunny places in which to eat and drink on the sea front. But the general effect was rather trippery: almost every shop in Etretat seemed to be selling postcards. The golf course, partly on neighbouring cliff tops, looked very inviting, and a golfing visitor could spend a happy day or two based at the 3-star Dormy House Hotel in its serene position, overlooking the sea.

A succession of roads through generally attractive, often wooded country brings you in an hour or two from Etretat on the coast to **Caudebec** on a beautiful bend of the Seine valley. This small town, backed by hills and facing towards the lovely Brotonne forest, is almost in the shadow of one of the only two splendid (toll) bridges (the other being the famous Tancarville) that span this great river below Rouen. The town has been largely rebuilt in recent times without damaging the mood and spirit of a place with a strong sense of history and of purpose. This seemed to be a friendly community with its fine old church and broad, well groomed riverside promenade lined with hotels of varying distinction. Some of these hotels have restaurants offering uninterrupted views across the river and countryside, notable among these being the 3-star Marine and the smaller 2-star Normandie. At the former I was to enjoy a fine if, to me, fairly expensive meal. The menu priced at 120F consisted of smoked salmon in perfect condition, a *filet mignon* in a delicate onion and lemon sauce and a delectable nougat ice. But this was worth paying for given the stylish service and impressive attention to detail, from the attractive china ware to the well presented *petits fours*, and high wide windows through which to enjoy the view.

Before this experience I had visited the smaller, delightful and even more attractively sited village of **Villequier** on its neighbouring bend of the river, backed by high wooded ground and with sweeping views across the water of woods and meadows. Pilots of the large ships on their way to Rouen embark here, and there are some pretty pubs by the riverside, a particularly inviting one being the 1-star Hôtel de France. And high above the village, on a lovely plateau with uninterrupted panoramas of the countryside up and beyond the river, is the château-type 4-star Domaine de Villequier, a large rather glamorous establishment with annexes and modern developments in excellent taste and a pleasant restaurant catering for the well-off customer. But time your visit carefully: this hotel, with good facilities for functions, plays host quite often to reunion dinners, weddings, seminars and conferences, not always the ideal accompaniment to a peaceful sojourn in the depths of the country: on such occasions, even in the best-run establishments, his territory curtailed in an unexpectedly alien ambience, the individual visitor may be led to feel that he does not count for much.

* * * *

Next morning, off the road to Rouen, I called at **Jumièges** for a brief visit to the ancient, partly ruined abbey of Notre Dame; and on the road again I paused in Duclair, a quite nice village distraught by the clatter and stench of queues of heavy lorries awaiting, embarking on or landing off a ferry which runs almost continuously from this point to the other side of the river.

As I entered **Rouen**, it was raining heavily. I worked my way across the city beside the river from west to east and rather hesitantly approached the steep climb to the Ste Catherine heights. It is worth getting lost a few times in the traffic system in search of the right exit from a complex roundabout by which the road for Pontoise detaches itself from the others before climbing and winding its way up the Bonsecours district to the famous viewing platform. My luck was in, for as the car at last came to rest in the small park beside the platform, the sky cleared and the sun came out.

Spread out at my feet, bisected by the broad, curving Seine, was this majestic city, its modern quarter on the left bank dominated by the local government buildings, its ancient, flanked by the handsome tree-lined boulevard beside the river, a darker mass punctuated by the tall spires of cathedral and churches. This is a vista that might well qualify for a 20th-century version of Christ's third temptation.

*   *   *   *

As a closer acquaintance was to confirm, Rouen has the style of a capital city and, at the same time, an intimacy which is all its own. I drove down from Ste Catherine, back part-way along the river and up the main, dead-straight artery, Rue Jeanne d'Arc, from Place du Théâtre to the railway station. This is a delightful building (by architect Adolphe Dervaux, opened in 1928) and, with its amusing frontage set off by a Gaudi-type clock tower, a clever foil to the more solemn and historic architecture that we know to be Rouen's pride and joy. Indeed, as I made my way up this busy street, I could glimpse to right and left some of the squares, narrow streets and alleyways which soon, with increasing wonder, I was to explore on foot.

For here, on a most generous scale, is a dazzling example of what imaginative and extensive restoration, allied with intelligent traffic management, can do to an ancient city, re-creating the past even to the extent of stripping down the newer façades of houses to reveal their medieval origins, as if exhuming valued skeletons. The maze of narrow, twisting and cobbled streets, nearly all of them pedestrianised, are now lined with shops, cafés and restaurants. A ghostly feeling, particularly after nightfall, unavoidable in a restored city centre as extensive as Rouen's, originally the bustling, cacophonous habitat of a cheek-by-jowl populace, but now effectively a museum piece, is mitigated by the fact that some Rouennais still live there, occupying the sometimes crumbling upper storeys above the shops; while claustrophobia is avoided by the way these old streets link a number of relatively open squares and gardens, which are often the settings for large buildings of beauty or distinction, like the cathedral, the almost equally imposing church of St Ouen, the City Hall and the museum. These areas display a mixture of old and new structures which blend well together and with their surroundings, adding to the dignity and variety of this remarkable city. And, along with a few locals going busily on foot about their daily business, you can have much of all this to yourself, as most tourists, after viewing the cathedral, tend to remain unadventurously in the vicinity of the Gros Horloge and Place du Vieux Marché, the latter despite its delightful modern church rather an anticlimax, and the former, in its improved surroundings no longer the conspicuous sight of earlier years.

Most Rouen hotels are in the older quarter in rather dark or cramped premises and, although the modern 4-star Frantel and the older 2-star Cathédrale are not unattractive, those by the station a few minutes walk away seem preferable. Notable among these are the busy 3-star Dieppe, well run with a personal touch by the Gueret family, with its friendly bar and good quality restaurant, the Quatre Saisons, and almost next door the starless, small hotel, Le Havre, with an inexpensive restaurant of excellent quality, presided over by its hospitable owner, Jean Carbonie; while the 2-star Astrid, right opposite the station, is more than adequate.

In the older quarter, both offering excellent value for money, are the lively Pascaline Brasserie, another Gueret enterprise, and in nearby Place Général de Gaulle, in my view Rouen's finest square, the more expensive and quieter Château d'O. The latter's well presented menu, for 70F, included fish paté, chicken in mushroom sauce and a heap of fresh strawberries.

If, from a tourist's point of view, this unique city has other flaws besides its disappointing hotels in the old quarter, it is the paucity of excursion facilities. Monsieur Rabany, regional director of tourism, assured me that improvements were intended, but meanwhile that great artery, the River Seine, is virtually neglected from the trippers' point of view. The city bus station could offer me neither information about local tours nor even a timetable of its services, and the information available at the railway station was not much easier to come by, owing to queues at the enquiry desk and the absence of displayed maps and timetables. Evidently it pays Rouen, having got the tourist in its midst, to make it hard for him to leave.

* * * *

Obstacles or not, it is always a wrench to quit Rouen; and for car drivers who have maps and can read road signs the obstacles are hardly insuperable. So, as the Summary at the start of this chapter proposes for day 3, having dined early in Rouen, we are bound by the fast main road for Dieppe and, after another night there and more sightseeing in the morning, to embark for England around lunch time. But another option is offered, time permitting, and in this case, with an extra day in hand, we may remain overnight in Rouen and use day 4 for an up-river reconnaissance, a cross-country drive to the coast, and perhaps a side trip to Le Tréport, before reaching Dieppe in the evening: thus we would run the homeward (day 4) programme a day late, on day 5.

One objective of the detour is **Les Andelys.** In this direction, both the river and its valley become narrower but, disappointingly, the countryside although still pretty becomes much more ordinary: on the whole rather less memorable than equivalent stretches of the rural Thames. Les Andelys struck me as a shapeless and rather forlorn place, the less than exciting main town being separated from its comparatively picturesque riverside portion by a rather boring avenue. One bright-looking spot down by the river was the 2-star Chaîne d'Or, a remarkable country pub-style restaurant, but when in search of a drink I walked in there after trying its terrace no-one seemed to mind very much whether I came or went; and after a quick look around the neighbourhood I duly went.

The slow road northward, leaving Neufchatel well over to the right, passes farming villages and the countryside is a pleasant relaxing mixture of woods, fields, low hills and shallow valleys. If you want to take in Le Tréport, however, the most direct route involves a half-way detour towards Neufchâtel and eventually, after Le Tréport, a fairly uninteresting road parallel to the coast. If earthy rumbustious resorts like, say, Clacton or Southend appeal to you make a detour to **Le Tréport** and share my pleasure in this cheerful place in its valley by the sea, with its river-mouth harbour, shingle beach and broad promenade lined with souvenir shops and cafés. It is reputedly the nearest seaside resort to Paris (though, in fact, slightly further away than Dieppe), enjoying a solid reputation for family outings and holidays. By mid morning on a summer Sunday the cars of the Parisian day trippers are nose-to-tail into the town and, until the return evening peak, Le Tréport is awash with visitors. But, so they say, this place seems to be able to absorb all-comers without limit, there being always somehow room to breath.

And so, finally, to Dieppe, completing both the circle and,

next morning, the local programme of visits described in the first part of this chapter. It remains to say only that Sealink's ferry service to Newhaven takes four hours, has straightforward car handling facilities and (with some sailings) efficient boat train connections at both ends and is run in a friendly way by what are, after all, the well-tried, old-established, cross-Channel 'professionals'. With French and British ships alternating you have the choice, if you wish, of eating, talking and acting French until the very last moments of your holiday.

Chapter 6 : A Norman Trail

Summary

In this chapter, travelling as light as possible, we use a quite straightforward succession of trains and buses to cover much of the coastline and its hinterland from Le Havre, our arrival port, along the Normandy Corniche including Honfleur and Deauville, to Caen and Bayeux, and returning home through Cherbourg.

Day	*Itineraries*
1st	Early morning, arrive **Le Havre** by overnight ferry from Southampton. Bus to rail station, leave baggage. Explore Le Havre all day, check in at hotel as convenient. (*Rec*: by station, France-Bourgogne, Terminus; in smarter central area, Angleterre, Foch.) Lunch, dine. (*Rec*: Station brasserie; in smarter area, Guillaume Tell brasserie; at Ste Adresse, and pricier, Nice-Havrais restaurant.)
2nd	Early or mid-morning, bus to **Honfleur.** Walkabout, snack lunch. Mid-afternoon, continue to **Deauville.** Check in at hotel for 2 nights. (*Rec*: near station, Continental; further on, inland, Fresnaye; on sea front, expensive failing special terms, Normandy, Royal.) Walkabout, dine. (*Rec*: Saratoga, Desirée-Deauville restaurants; Chantilly, Drakkar brasseries.)
3rd	Short day trips: by train to **Lisieux**, on foot to **Trouville.** Complete Deauville walkabout.
4th	After breakfast, bus to **Cabourg.** Walkabout, continue by lunchtime bus to **Caen.** Explore this city, having checked in at hotel near station. (*Rec*: France.) Lunch, dine. (*Rec*: station, Royal, La Coupole brasseries; Assiette or the

more expensive Relais des Gourmets restaurants.)

5th Mid-morning, train to **Bayeux.** Walkabout, snack lunch, continue by mid-afternoon train to **Cherbourg.** Taxi to hotel. (*Rec*: convenient for ferry, fairly pricey, Sofitel; more central, less expensive, France, Grand, Torgistops.) Walkabout, dine. (*Rec*: Paris, Vauban restaurants; Théâtre brasserie.)

6th Complete walkabout. After lunch, embark in ferry for Southampton, arriving early evening.

A tour of Normandy must be incomplete without sampling the Manche/Cotentin (Cherbourg) Peninsula. By adding 2 or 3 days to the foregoing, the following is possible, mainly by train, partly by bus:

5th Mid-morning, train to **Bayeux.** Walkabout, snack lunch, return to Caen mid-afternoon. Change trains for **Argentan** for brief visit, continue by train to arrive **Granville** for dinner. Check in at hotel. (*Rec*: Des Bains, Michelet.) Eat nearby. (*Rec*: Normandy-Chaumière, or any likely brasserie on road from station into town centre.)

6th Explore Granville. Early afternoon, train (via Folligny) or bus to **Avranches.** Check in at hotel. (*Rec*: Croix d'Or, by steep footpath from station.) Walkabout, dine at hotel (or further on, at Auberge St Michel).

7th	Mid-morning, train to **Coutances.** Walkabout, possible side trip to Coutainville. Evening, bus to arrive Cherbourg for dinner. . .	**or**	Remain in Avranches or take side trip by air or road to Mont-St-Michel. Early evening, train to **Coutances**. Check in at hotel. (*Rec*: Grand.) Dine at hotel, walkabout.
8th	Complete walkabout. After lunch, embark in		Mid-morning, bus to arrive **Cherbourg** lunchtime. . .

ferry for Southampton, arriving early evening.

9th — Complete walkabout. After lunch, embark in ferry for Southampton, arriving early evening.

As the foregoing itineraries are a little too long to qualify for the reduced-rate return fares usually available to foot passengers, there may be no great advantage in using the same ferry company for both outward and homeward cross-Channel voyages. While the Southampton–Havre route is worked by Townsend Thoresen as well as by P & O, only the former provides a Cherbourg–Southampton service, but Townsend Thoresen plies Cherbourg–Portsmouth as well; and there is also a Cherbourg–Weymouth Sealink service. The afternoon ferry to Southampton arrives in time for a fast evening train from the town station to London.

Author's Narrative

A dawn arrival in Le Havre by one of the overnight ferries from Southampton can be a bleak affair. Apart from a range of green hills behind the city, the general effect is grey. From the P & O berth in the huge dock area it is quite a step to where life begins, and the route is not inviting. Townsend Thoresen does this rather better, its terminal being on a relatively pleasant quayside only a quarter-mile or so from the heart of the city though the side-by-side rail and coach stations, being slighty off centre, are not within comfortable walking distance: however, a bus to and from the station connects with most early morning arrivals and late evening departures of these ferries.

The core of this great maritime and industrial city is its enormous main square, Place Hôtel-de-Ville, focus of the great work of Auguste Perret by whose bold scheme of reconstruction Le

Havre rose again from the ashes of World War II: Le Havre was the worst damaged of all Continental ports. Anyone interested in the urban environment and, particularly, in town planning on a large scale should spend a day or two here, starting in the main square, and preferably on foot, to appreciate this remarkable man's legacy.

Now, with the passage of time, most of it is looking good, but some, alas, remains bad and the worst, perhaps, is the too-vast open area of Place Hôtel-de-Ville itself. The feeling is windswept and, on wet days, shelter is lacking; at a distance, despite a foreground of gardens, the surrounding buildings look grim, barracks-like, as well as remote. And the proportions of this area are generally more suited to a processional approach to a royal palace than to the forecourt of a provincial town hall, although Perret's town hall in Le Havre is, indeed, on the scale of a royal palace.

But the building looks too institutional: it lacks grace and vitality and, for a grand design, its setting is not convincing; and one feels that Perret, affected by the socialist ideals of his era (he died in 1954) was paying too much tribute to devolved democracy. It is a shame that, at such a moment, a fine city like Le Havre could find no idol worthier than a branch of local government: in Plymouth's equivalent scheme due homage is well paid to the city's history, personified by Drake, the handsome new ¾-mile north-south avenue, Armada Way, culminating respectfully at the foot of The Hoe.

Perret's scheme, breaking many of the bounds of convention, shows great integrity and determination as well as imagination; and he has not forgotten that cities are, or ought to be, for people. For example, a closer look shows that, on the main square and in street after street around it, Perret provided living accommodation for all classes in attractive blocks of flats above most of the shops and some of the offices, and the lights in row upon row of windows at night give a feeling of warmth and friendliness lacking in British rebuilt city centres. Another good feature is the shelter afforded to shoppers and pedestrians by continuous overhanging balconies, and in some important streets, such as Rue de Paris, by colonnades and avenues of trees. While many of the shops are conveniently situated, however, the shopping area as a whole, punctuated by the wide streets and squares, is rather spread out, so that cohesion and a sense of intimacy are lacking. But the plan is certainly a boon to motorists who can not only drive from A to B in uncongested comfort but can park almost anywhere at any time and, as the trees planted at the time of reconstruction grow large and, with surprising warmth and dignity, the concrete façades of the buildings mature, the brave new dream at last comes true.

*   *   *   *

Several buildings are of particular interest, including Perret's most astonishing creation, St Joseph Church, which stands between the main square and the nearby yacht harbour. The stained glass windows are set both in the side walls and all the way up the soaring tower itself, while the seating, in comfortable cinema-style chairs, is arranged like an amphitheatre around the altar, a starkly simple feature, like a conference table, right in the middle beneath the tower. But, striking though this is, it cannot quite compare with one of Le Havre's few surviving ancient buildings, Notre Dame cathedral. There is also the impressive, modern Fine Arts Museum on the sea front which, with its high windows facing the ocean, also deserves inspection.

For recreation, besides the plage area, there is above and behind the town, approached through a magnificent road tunnel, the Montgeon Forest. The adjoining heights offer a panorama of passing ships, the city behind its endless harbour and the open sea, blue now, as it should be, under the mid-day sun. Up here, in quiet comfort, in their flats and houses, live some of the middle-class families, while further over, still on high ground, looking south along the beath, is the picturesque district of Ste Adresse, with its fort, smart old villas and choice of restaurants and cafés.

Of these, the most distinguished is Nice-Havrais, a suave, somewhat formal restaurant with sweeping views across the harbour entrance. At the fairly high price of 135F, in almost lonely splendour, I was served a fine meal of shrimp pancake, turbot in a raspberry-vinegar sauce, a good cheese board, and profiteroles with ice cream in a Benedictine sauce. There is also a very inviting and well run brasserie, Guillaume Tell, with high, wide windows overlooking Place Hôtel-de-Ville. My excellent lunch there, for 65F, included a main course of fillet of salmon in a sorrel and lemon sauce, the cheeses and desserts also being first class. The hotels in Le Havre are no great shakes, most of them seeming to be below the average of their respective classes. The 2-star Foch, situated on a quiet corner close to the main square, is friendly, and the nearby Angleterre, also 2-star is acceptable. The 3-star France-Bourgogne and 2-star Terminus opposite the main railway station, with its good-value brasserie, are adequate at a commercial hotel standard.

* * * *

Next day, some 24 hours after our dawn landing in Le Havre, we made our way to the coach station to seek out and board the Caen-bound Courriers-Normands bus. There are usually two morning departures, one around breakfast time, the other mid-morning, the service being less frequent on Sundays. The bus sets off through industrial suburbs, crosses high over the Seine estuary by the magnificent Tancarville bridge and, an hour later, reaches **Honfleur.** Here we alight and, failing facilities at the bus stop, negotiate a baggage-leaving arrangement over coffee at the adjoining café, the aim being to resume our westward journey on the mid-afternoon bus.

Honfleur has long been a favourite place with the British, not least with deep-water yachtsmen. The famous enclosed port is very small, the yacht basin cramped and undistinguished, and the surrounding quaysides, some of them not free of road traffic, are not large or striking enough to hold the interest for very long, and I found the generally dun colour of the high buildings lining them oddly gloomy: climate apart, Honfleur does not begin to be in the same league as St Tropez.

There are some inviting restaurants and adequate hotels on and near the port, and there is the extraordinary wooden church of Ste Catherine, among other fine buildings which include the town's Musée Boudin, but the narrow shopping streets are over-embellished with commercial signs and I found rather too many galleries and studios selling paintings of the locality of disappointing quality.

Unluckily, Honfleur is today only a small oasis of antiquity in a proliferating desert of industrial and commercial development, the views from the seaside promenade being dominated by the apparatus of large-scale modern industry on both sides of the Seine estuary. However, fifty million Englishmen cannot be wrong, and I will bow my head and say no more.

* * * *

From Honfleur, it is only a half-hour bus ride to **Deauville**, along a road which skirts the sometimes beautiful, occasionally dramatic coastline known as the **Corniche Normande.** This once-glamorous and still spruce villa-playground country consists of a series of village resorts interspersed with farmland and orchards, hills and valleys, tree-lined cliffs and beaches, until at last, on the final descent through Trouville, you catch signs of Deauville spread out like a magic carpet on its flat green plain by the sea.

The main bus stop here is next to the rail station and, having deposited our baggage, we set off in search of accommodation. The less expensive hotels are to be found mainly on or near Avenue de la République, a tree-lined boulevard which carries a large share of through traffic. Just off this street, facing the station, is the cheerful 2-star Continental, while in the boulevard itself, among others worth considering, are the cosy 3-star Fresnaye and the 2-star Nid d'Eté, the latter being a popular venue for resident cookery courses. Deauville also offers a number of short-stay holiday flats including the Résidence Orion's fairly new, well run furnished studio flatlets, with balconies, which sleep up to four people, but only on lets of at least three days.

On the sea front, about ten minutes' walk from the station, apart from the modern 3-star PLM on its island site in the middle of Deauville's hugely lavish new yacht harbour, the hotels seem to be only, or mainly, in the 5-star bracket, led by the quietly splendid Normandy open all the year round and its more grandiose and mildly raffish neighbour the Royal, the two separated by the gleaming white summer casino. But these two hotels, along with their equally plush sister further inland, the Golf, will be pleased to have you for three nights or more, breakfast and service included, in a luxurious twin-bedded room overlooking the sea, at little more than 3-star prices (in 1982, 200F a head). In my view, this is the best bargain of its kind along the whole northern littoral of France.

* * * *

Deauville on the face of it looks almost as though time has stood still for half a century. Even the quietly spacious rail station, opened in 1931, seems like a film set awaiting the actors for some sophisticated romance of that period. The leading hotels and many of the villas in their garden settings, most of them in almost overbearing neo-Norman-Gothic style, are defiant relics of the days when rich people, their families and their servants, arriving ostentatiously for a short summer season in their seaside mansions or hotel suites, were happy to flaunt their wealth, secure in the belief that the world would ever be their oyster.

Although fashionable race meetings, golf tournaments, festivals, gala evenings and other palmier-day baubles continue to be among the high season's highlights, Deauville has adapted skilfully to the times. While at all seasons still a refuge for stylish, well-heeled Parisians, it caters admirably with refined verve and confidence for the rest of us as well. Albeit with rather fewer open in the winter than the summer, there are, besides smart shops, stores and markets for those needing to be careful with their money. There is also a remarkable variety of eating places, from the opulent lunch-only Ciro's by the beach to a number of merry, inexpensive brasseries and bistros towards the station end of the town. It is also a very pleasant place just to stroll about in.

On the edge of the broad, spotlessly clean sandy beach, fronting the famous Planche promenade, besides Ciro's, there are several cheaper bars and brasseries, with indoor and outdoor seating, all of them thronged with visitors at high summer weekends. Bathers willing to pay a little for their dip have a choice between the magnificent covered sea-water swimming pool on the common behind the Planche and a hired sun umbrella on the beach with wind curtain and all accessories necessary for their comfort, including lunch with wine brought by an attendant on a tray, complete with non-disposable cutlery, glass, china and napkin. No sign here of the dejectedly shuffling Sunday-morning crowds to be found on a typical English sea-front, hoping gloomily that the rain will hold off before the pubs open. The Deauville crowds, whole families on a day's outing, young men with their girls, the elderly, the rich and not so rich, all bring a sense of fun and vitality.

For dinner in the grand manner the 5-star hotels have splendid, rather expensive restaurants with cuisines of a high gastronomic standard, but less pricey, and just behind the casino is the quietly elegant Saratoga restaurant, which extends into a pleasant garden in good weather and has a few bedrooms at 2-star level of comfort. For a cheaper meal in livelier company, and still in the fashionable area, try La Drakkar brasserie; and cheaper still, rather nearer the station, is the simpler and very enjoyable Chantilly (Chez Noë) brasserie. A block away is the entertaining Desirée-Deauville, with its amusing Ottoman-cum-Art-Deco ambience; while beside that is the slightly more up-market and conventional Chez Camillo.

*　　*　　*　　*

A stone's throw on the other side of the local river, the Touques, crossed by a ferry adjoining the marina or by a road bridge, is the sister resort of **Trouville**, but this, being under a different administration, is not usually featured on Deauville maps and leaflets, Deauville being similarly ignored in Trouville's tourist literature. But holiday-makers soon learn to ignore such bureaucratic piffle, the two resorts being useful foils one to another, the visitor to Deauville enjoying an outing and, perhaps, some cheaper shopping in earthier Trouville, and the tourist in Trouville an evening's stroll in more *soigné* Deauville. Only French Railways, with careful tact, seem to have made the best of both worlds: the station serving both places is in Deauville, but only just; and its name, officially, is Trouville-Deauville.

In its picturesque setting, Trouville is the older and more bustling and down-market resort of the two, much of it on high ground with many remnants of once classy villas. It has its own version of a Planche promenade but, alas, it is not a very inspiring one. Although it has a wide variety of shops and eating places and one imposing hotel, the newly re-opened 3-star Bellevue facing the casino across the busy square, I found little here that I could not enjoy as well if not better on the Deauville side of the Touques.

*　　*　　*　　*

Using Deauville as a base, it is easy to make side trips, whether by bus along the coast in both directions, or inland, by bus or train, to **Lisieux.** On its half-hour journey the train calls at Pont-l'Evêque, home of one of Normandy's famous cheeses; and if it is a local train it will stop at the north end of Lisieux at the nicely-named station, La Gare du Jardin. From here it is a one-mile walk through the city, including most of the principal sights, to the main station at the south end, where refreshments may be obtained while awaiting the train back to Deauville.

Walking south you soon reach the lovely public gardens, adjacent to the cathedral and, in the old bishop's palace, the Palais de Justice. The cathedral, in the French Gothic style, is outstanding although the famous Paradise Door ceiling is disappointing.

Heading west along the boulevards Carnot and Pasteur the flavour of Lisieux begins to emerge, old timbered houses in their narrow alleys being much in evidence, the reconstruction blending tactfully with the ancient buildings. At the end of the Boulevard Pasteur, the Musée de Vieux Lisieux is situated in a very elderly timbered house, its regional pottery and costumes being of interest. Eastward from the museum, along Rue Henri Chéron, you re-cross the river Touques into the centre of Lisieux.

To your right, after passing the rows of modern shops, any of the small streets will lead you past the Eglise Saint-Jacques, the main bus station and the inviting 1-star hotel Lisieux, to the part of Lisieux connected with the remarkable life of Sainte Thérèse. Thousands of pilgrims come here every year on her account. Further east, across the railway and up some steep steps, is the Basilica Sainte-Thérèse, an imposing modern building, ornate inside, with an impressive view of Lisieux and the surrounding countryside from the terrace on which Pope Jean-Paul II celebrated mass.

* * * *

After two nights in Deauville we continue along the coast towards Caen, this section, the **Côte Fleurie**, whether viewed from road or railway, although lower lying, being in many ways lusher and prettier than that of the Corniche. Two particularly attractive places are the small resort of **Houlgate**, contained between the open sea, the mouth of an estuary and surrounding woodland, and Cabourg, a larger, more elaborate town separated from Houlgate by **Dives**, now the railhead, where William the Conqueror once assembled his fleet to invade England.

Cabourg, where we left our bus in mid-morning, is a quiet, respectable, once elegant resort with a street pattern which, on the map, resembles an open lady's fan. Its trim villas in their gardens have charm and on the sea-front, at the point where all the ribs of the fan meet, stands the 4-star Grand Hotel and the large casino which gives promise of a bit of high life. But there is a *fin de siècle* feeling about Cabourg and when I visited the town in mid-summer a businessmen's conference in the hotel was one of the few signs of life, high or low.

The sea front, with fine coastal views, is pleasant to walk on and the tree-lined main street, Avenue de la Mer, has an acceptable variety of shops, bars and bistros, while at its inland end, by the main bus stop, and not far from the railway station just across the river in Dives, is a nice arrangement of church and public gardens. Next time, try Cabourg for a quiet overnight visit and savour what is left of the leisurely pace of a once much-favoured watering place. For a community of little more than 3,000 people it has a surprising number of hotels, from 4 to 1-star; and if you are carless and cannot make it all the way to the sea front, the 2-star Paris, 300 yards up the main street, might do you very well.

This time, however, after only a two to three hour stay, we resumed our journey to **Caen** by the lunchtime bus, alighting in the efficient new coach station of that city. Having checked our baggage in the next-door rail station, we may well wonder what brought us here for, while most French cities are well approached through their station, Caen is not. Its main station is a cramped and undistinguished building and the terrace of modern buildings across the adjoining square, including a number of hotels and cafés, does Caen no credit architecturally.

We turned right and then right again beneath the railway bridge into the city's main thoroughfare, a wide boulevard, Rue St Jean, the upper end of which, a kilometre away, frames the handsome castle. On your left, before crossing the river Orne, is the very acceptable 2-star hotel France while further up, as you enter the city's main shopping district, a wider choice of accommodation and other amenities becomes available. But most of these attractions are quite a step from the station which has no exit on its city side.

Its station area apart Caen, thanks to sound city planning and the attractive local stone, has done an exemplary job in rebuilding itself following the 1944 devastations. Unlike Rouen, today's Caen is mainly a reconstruction, a new town in a traditional style, rather than a restoration. Over a large area Rouen has been fastidiously loyal enough to its past to re-create faithfully the heart of a former city, but in Caen, while the old castle and the two famous abbeys on their high ground dominate the skyline, the surviving ancient quarter is more fragmented. The overall impression is of a handsome 20th-century city aware of but not overawed by its history.

The modern streets and buildings blend well with their surroundings, the urban pattern broken by squares and waterways, trees and gardens, promenades and precincts, all providing a dignified yet cheerful setting for the people. And Caen is very much a city for work as well as play: the docks and basins in the centre serve as a reminder of this community's commercial importance, and the proximity of shopping streets and office blocks to some of the historic buildings hint that there is no lifeblood without trade and business.

Of the ancient religious buildings the two abbeys (the one aux Hommes and the other aux Dames), a kilometre apart at either side of the city centre, the chateau, including the main museum and art gallery, and the less conspicuous but still beautiful church of St Pierre, all deserve a visit. There are some attractive old squares in the castle area and nearby a pedestrianised shopping district of no special distinction but here, on a quiet corner, may be found one of Caen's leading hotels, the 3-star Moderne, while close by, overlooking Place République, is the welcoming 2-star Royal with its lively, well-run street-side bar and brasserie. Another recommended bar and brasserie, also in modern style and in this case occupying two and a half floors of a building facing St Pierre, is La Coupole. If you want to eat more conventionally, try the Michelin-rosetted Relais des Gourmets in its garden setting, L'Assiette on the first floor by the Palais de Justice or the station buffet.

*　*　*　*

Next morning, our fifth of the present trip, we caught a train for Bayeux. If we had been following the basic (shortest) itinerary, as outlined at the start of this chapter, and intended to continue by an afternoon train to Cherbourg, we should have had our baggage with us. In fact, we left it at Caen station to which we shall return briefly in the afternoon in pursuit of the extended (9-day) journey.

The ride to **Bayeux** by rail takes only twenty minutes and the station is on the southern edge of the town centre within half a mile of the principal sights. Decisions made here have determined the history of England; and the extraordinary story of Harold, who on the instructions of Edward the Confessor came to swear allegiance to William of Normandy only later to provoke the Norman invasion by proclaiming himself King, is told in the famous 11th-century tapestry. Coachloads queue dutifully to take their turn to view this linen frieze, with the help of an audio-earphone commentary.

Out of range of the excess of traffic passing through the handsome shopping streets of St Malo, St Martin and St Jean, Bayeux has a wonderful tranquility. These shopping streets form part of N13 and towards each extremity lie the best hotels and restaurants, mostly well set back from the road including, to the east, the old 3-star hostelry, Lion d'Or which attracts many English visitors.

The Norman Gothic cathedral of Notre Dame is quite glorious, and Bayeux has a score of exceptional houses within their own courtyards. It is a pleasure to wander from the Dean's

House, which contains the tapestry, across to the 18th-century bishopric, now the Baron Gérard Museum with its porcelain and lace, down Rue des Cuisiniers into Rue St Martin, where you will find the tourist office in a timber-framed house. Beyond this is a choice of streets: Rue Franche, with its 15th-century manor house and the 18th-century Crespillière Mansion; or Rue Général de Dais, down which you can walk past the elms of Place Général de Gaulle and back, via Rue Bourbesneur, to the fine 13th-century south transept of the cathedral.

If time allows, Bayeux, which itself has an interesting museum depicting aspects of the Battle for Normandy in 1944, offers a convenient base from which to make an excursion to the **D-Day Beaches.** Coach tours are sometimes available, and otherwise a car will be needed.

There are five named beaches extending about fifty miles westward from a position between Cabourg and the mouth of the Orne to half-way up the east side of the Cotentin (Cherbourg) peninsula. The first three (Sword, Juno, Gold) were in the British-Canadian sector and the next two (Omaha, Utah) in the American sector, Bayeux being five miles due south of the boundary between the two groups of beaches. On the British side, close to this boundary, is Arromanches which, besides containing the most substantial of the various D-Day museums, has the best vantage point from which to see what remains of the famous Mulberry harbours. A few miles away, on the American side, are two of the largest war cemeteries in this area, one American (near St Laurent), the other German (at La Cambe); and a good deal further on, at Ste Mère Eglise, a target of the paratroopers, is the airborne museum, as well as the church steeple featured so dramatically in the film, *The Longest Day*.

* * * *

In mid-afternoon, we returned by train to Caen where we changed almost at once for **Argentan**, an agricultural town thirty-five miles to the south in the heart of inland Normandy. The couple of hours' wait before continuing westward to Granville is enough for a walk around this plainly rebuilt but cheerful, well tended place, with its two fine churches, both still being restored following the war damage. In these parts is France's national stud and there is much racehorse activity. The farmland, often part of wealthy estates, looks sleek and fertile, and attractive timber-framed houses and parks are a feature of the scenery.

On its way towards Granville the train heads through quieter, partly-wooded *bocage* country, while to north and south are the more picturesque hills and valleys of, respectively, the 'alpine' district known as Suisse Normande and the spa country of which the inland resort of Bagnoles de L'Orne is the focus. As the hour for dinner approaches, the Atlantic air in our nostrils, we arrive in **Granville**, terminus of this little-known secondary railway line from Paris.

This bracing, once-fortified port and resort, built on and around a vast slab or rock jutting into the sea, calls itself the 'Monaco of the North'. The modern station building looks attractive and there is a selection of fairly ordinary cafés nearby in the busy main road and shopping street which leads to the town centre, the Normandy-Chaumière brasserie being a good bet for dinner.

On the north side of the town there is excellent walking through the Christian Dior gardens and a residential area above the rocky-sandy beach. At the west end of the beach lie the 2-star hotels Des Bains, which is modern with sea views, and Michelet which is older; a health centre, a casino and more cafés. Further west, a steep climb up steps to the ramparts of the very attractive upper town offers views northward along the coast, including the fine sandy beach at nearby Donville, the peaceful narrow streets of old Granville culminating in a lovely square around the handsome 15th-century church of Notre Dame. The ramparts end here but beyond, past barracks, the walk may be continued to

Pointe du Roc on its bleak, high cliffs above the ocean. Along the south side of this promontory, immediately below the old town, is the large commercial and fishing port and yacht harbour from which day trips run to Jersey and the Iles de Chausey.

After a night and a full morning in this enjoyable place, with its varied character and amenities, you may continue a short way southward by direct bus or by train, changing at Folligny, to the charming old town of **Avranches**. Built on high ground, it may be approached by a short, very steep climb up a footpath from the off-centre rail station. But the arriving pedestrian will do better to take the bus, which has its main stop right in the middle of the town. The main hotel district is in and around the modernised Place Général Patton by the southern edge of the central area. The most attractive hotel, with a pleasant garden, is the 2-star Croix d'Or, but the 2-star Auberge St Michel is very adequate besides being, perhaps, the best spot in Avranches for an evening meal.

The main features of this agreeable place are its Jardin des Plantes, a beautifully kept garden well known for its panoramic view across the flat estuary to Mont-St-Michel, a museum, a handsome cathedral, a small castle, lively streets not scarred by war, and a number of pleasant buildings, such as the Town Hall. But for many its main attraction may be its proximity to **Mont-St-Michel**, possibly the most famous of all French tourist sights outside Paris and, inevitably, the target of an almost endless but skilfully handled succession of coach parties. This fantastically picturesque abbey on its great ramparted rock is surrounded, at high tide, by water. The dense, cascading architecture of a minute terraced city of ancient houses on steep streets and steps is so exceptional that anyone within easy reach dare not give it a miss. And Avranches, at a mere 14 miles, is near enough to make a detour there: if not by coach or bus then, yes, *by air*. You can take a plane from Avranches airport, a few miles south of the town, which, all being well, and the tide being not too high, offers there-and-back excursions for visitors with limited time to spare. The tourist office near the Avranches Town Hall and bus station knows which method is feasible on any given day.

In the early evening of our seventh day we left Avranches by direct train for **Coutances**, arriving as the dinner gongs were sounding. Here, by the station, is the 2-star Grand hotel, not exactly grand but pleasant enough for dinner and a short overnight stay.

So, up early next day for a visit to the exceptional hill-top cathedral, an outstanding example of Norman Gothic, with its fabulous lantern tower. If time permits a breath of sea air at Coutainville, nine miles to the west, the leading resort of western Manche on the long stretch of coast between Granville and Carteret, might not come amiss. Otherwise you should proceed to Cherbourg by the mid-morning bus, which you will find at the rail station.

* * * *

The two-hour journey to Cherbourg crosses gently undulating country, a landscape of scattered church spires, country houses and farm buildings, broken by occasional villages of charm and character of which Lessay, with its old Romanesque abbey, and St Sauveur le Vicomte and Briquebec, with their castles, are of interest.

At lunch time the bus, having passed through typically industrial suburbs, comes to rest at its terminus in an undistinguished forecourt, shared with the rail station, on the southern edge of central **Cherbourg.** We are at once aware that the heart of this important seafaring city is water, its main part being built around the enclosed basins of the extensive port. Post-war rebuilding along the quays is generally in a hard, forbidding and uneven style: and with traffic, mainly business and commercial, heavy lorries and all, tending to be funnelled along the quays to the few dock-end crossings we are made aware that Cherbourg, at least in working hours, is mainly a place of toil and turmoil, and hardly for a moment at rest. Away from the dock area there are remnants of the older town but the winding streets, where they have not been pedestrianised, are so conjested by all the converging and diverging road traffic, as well as by shoppers and trippers hemmed in to the narrow pavements, that there is not much pleasure in exploring them. The quieter, rather grey-looking sea-front, effectively separated from its natural element by the harbour's outer ring of break waters, is punctuated by wharves, arsenals or warehouses. There is generous provision for yacht berths in basins near the sea front and it is possible to stroll along some of these quaysides. It is still better to await the evening before attempting more than a partial meander.

The ferry terminals, on the far side of the central area from the rail and bus stations, are within a few minutes' walk of the centre. Alongside the terminals is Cherbourg's leading hotel, the Sofitel, a particularly ugly modern building but with a friendly staff, pleasant views and all the amenities to be expected of a 4-star hotel with the needs of today's businessmen in mind. Then, in the midst of all the down-town hubbub, there are the very acceptable France and Grand, 2-star and 1-star respectively, while around the corner from these, in a less claustrophobic spot near the beach, is the quaint 2-star Torgistops.

Place Général de Gaulle in the old quarter contains a pleasant modern brasserie, the Théâtre, a good vantage point from which to watch the world go by. On Thursdays a flower market joins the ice cream and pancake booths which do good business both with visitors and with locals waiting for the town buses. The fruit market, cheese stalls and cheap clothing tables extend into the next square, the rebuilt Place Divette, where the Thomas Henry Museum has just reopened in the new arts complex. There is a great variety of small shops in this corner of Cherbourg but for food shopping car drivers may prefer to use the hypermarket near the ferry terminals.

By all accounts the leading restaurant in Cherbourg is the Vauban on the quayside, but during my visit there I preferred the Café de Paris almost next door, with its high windows giving close-up views of the passing heavy lorries, the slow-moving tourists and glimpses of yacht masts and other maritime abracadabra. Before embarking for England on our ninth and final day we had a splendid lunch in this cheerful restaurant, paying 70F for an excellent *soupe de poissons*, an *escalope normande*, a generous salad and a succulent almond tart.

* * * *

From Cherbourg in 1982 there were ferries to Weymouth by Sealink and to Portsmouth and Southampton by Townsend Thoresen. The afternoon sailings reached Weymouth or Southampton in time for an evening train to Waterloo. When on the morning of departure I had bought tickets for the Townsend Thoresen 1530 service to Southampton, the office had said we could board any time from 1400: in the event, however, embarkation did not begin until 1510 by which time the terminal had long been crowded beyond its seating capacity. Our ship, the *Viking Valiant*, was pretty full including large contingents of roaming school-age children but it was well run by a cheerful, hard-working crew and, except in the restaurant and café which were always busy, there seemed to be ample space for all.

At Southampton, however, not so good: herded cheek-by-jowl into a small ill-ventilated lobby at the entrance to the car decks so that the stewards could have a clear run with their cleaning gear at the lounges we, the non-motorists, children, pensioners, hand baggage and all, were kept standing for over twenty minutes until every vehicle was off the ship, before being allowed to walk briefly across a corner of the car deck to the ramp of escape: not the ideal end to a happy voyage.

However, as I hope these last two chapters make clear, Normandy in all its beauty and variety is *well* worth the trials and tribulations that getting there and back may sometimes entail.

Chapter 7 : Wars and Battlefields

Much of the history of northern France has been concerned with war, and, indeed, throughout the centuries this region has had more than its fair share of invasion, expeditions, battles, with widespread bloodshed and destruction. Time and again cities and agricultural land have been laid waste, restored, destroyed again, so that almost every village remembers conflict, sometimes from centuries past, often within living memory.

There follows a selection of principal war-like events, divided into two sections, the first pre-20th century and the second dealing with the two World Wars..

Section 1. Pre-20th Century

BC	France inhabited by different tribes.
58–51	Roman conquest of France follcenturies of occupation. Caesar is reputed to have launched his invasion of Britain from Wissant, just south of Calais, in 55 BC.
AD	
5th–7th centuries	Immigration of British Celts to Brittany.
9th–10th centuries	Norsemens' destructive invasions of north-west France, halted by ceding territories around the Seine, hence the name Normandy.
1066	William the Conqueror's invasion of Britain with a fleet prepared at Dives and launched from St Valéry-sur-Somme.
1337–1453	The Hundred Years War between England and France. Even during short periods of

	uneasy peace, mercenaries from both sides pillaged and murdered their way around the countryside, terrorising the inhabitants and destroying their livelihood. Important events include: 1346, Battle of Crécy; 1347, Siege of Calais; 1415, Battle of Agincourt when an English army of 6,000 defeated 12,000 French, many of whom were mounted; 1417, Siege of Rouen; 1420, Siege of Troyes, which recognized Henry V as King of France; 1431, trial and execution of Joan of Arc at Rouen. After this, France gradually won back its lost territories and the war petered out until, in 1558, England gave up Calais, its last toe-hold in France.
16th-century	Wars of Religion between Catholics and Huguenots, the latter gaining freedom of worship in the Edict of Nantes in 1598 until this was rescinded by Louis XIV nearly 100 years later.
1520–1659	Emperor Charles V of Austria besieged much of Artois with Spanish troops brought from his territories in the Netherlands: after this occupation many towns in north-eastern France were fortified by Vauban.
1789	The Revolution.
1793–1794	The Reign of Terror.
1803–04	Napoleon stationed enormous army at Boulogne with a view to invading England. The port was enlarged to accommodate 2000.
1870–71	Franco-Prussian War, when parts of north-east France were occupied by Prussian forces.

Section 2. The Two World Wars

Much of the worst fighting in World War I (1914–18) took place in the trenches of north-east France and just across the frontier with Belgium. The casualty statistics of this war, 'great' indeed in terms of misery and suffering, make chilling reading, the bleakest tragedy being that so many died for so little territorial gain. The Battle of the Somme, fought from July 1916 is a prime example: by the beginning of December, the Allies had advanced all of seven miles along a twenty-mile front at a cost of 420,000 British and Commonwealth, 195,000 French and 650,000 German casualties. By the end of the war, France alone had lost almost 1½ million soldiers and half a million civilians, while a further three-quarters of a million were permanently disabled, and even today some ten bodies a year are unearthed by unsuspecting tractors.

World War II (1939–45) brought renewed devastation to a region that had only just rebuilt its cities and stabilised its industrial and agricultural heritage. During this conflict virtually the whole of the northern French coastline and much of its hinterland came under fire, notable events including the Dunkerque evacuation (26 May–4 June 1940) when some 350,000 men, including 120,000 French, were brought to England in an armada of 860 mostly small boats; the Allied raid on Dieppe (August 1942) when out of 5,000 men (mostly Canadians) sent by sea to capture the port some 3,500 failed to return; and (from 6 June 1944) the legendary Normandy landings when, as part of a mammoth international feat of arms, American, Canadian and British troops landed successfully on code-named stretches of the Normandy coastline. Some 2,500 Allies were killed in this operation.

Although the outcome of World War II gave victory to the Allies, the manner of its achievement once again devastated many French communities. At St Lô in July 1944, 4,200 tons of bombs were dropped in 90 minutes over an area 1½ × 2½ miles, and Abbeville, Havre, Cherbourg, Caen, Lisieux (to name but a few of the stricken cities) were virtually razed to the ground. By the time hostilities ceased northern France had borne the brunt of a destruction which had damaged some 2 million French houses, half a million of them beyond repair, decimated the railways and put nine-tenths of road vehicles out of action.

Today, reminders of the two World Wars are everywhere. Trenches and dug-outs have been preserved while museums and displays of other fighting abound in most of the main battle areas. The most poignant legacy of the fighting, however, is the hundreds of war cemeteries scattered around the countryside. Many of those from World War I are to be found around Arras and Amiens, together with some important free-standing memorials including those at Vimy (where over 60,000 Canadians and many thousands of Frenchmen are remembered), Thiepval (commemorating the missing of the Somme) and Villers-Bretonneux (the Australian National Memorial). Northern France has, indeed, become a truly international graveyard. Like George V in Flanders in 1922, we too must wonder 'whether there can be more potent advocates of peace upon earth through the years to come, than this massed multitude of silent witnesses to the desolation of war'.

Among the facilities for visitors are those offered by Major and Mrs Holt (Oak House, Oak Hill, Woodnesborough, Sandwich, Kent. Tel 0304 612248). Cemeteries containing the remains of Commonwealth Citizens are cared for by the Commonwealth War Graves Commission (2 Marlow Road, Maidenhead, Berkshire SL6 7DX) who can provide information on request.

Chapter 8 : Art and Architecture

For most British travellers to France Paris remains the first place of artistic pilgrimage but the region covered by this book, from the Belgian frontier to west Brittany, is at least as rich as any other area of France both in its public art collections housed in fine buildings and in its picturesque places where famous artists, French and British, once worked and put on record some of the region's exceptional scenery and architecture.

For the inquisitive tourist it can be a refreshing and rewarding experience to approach art in this way: to go to an artist's place of birth or inspiration, to walk where he walked and sit where he painted, and then with luck or perseverance discover a related work, maybe just a sketch, in the dusty corner of some out-of-the-way provincial gallery. Such experiences, besides giving new interest to the holiday, may evoke that sharp, self-satisfied pleasure of personal discovery that eludes the most competent guided tour or audio commentary.

Brittany, for example, can boast international art colonies which sprang up in the 1870s at Cancale, Concarneau, Douarnenez and Pont-Aven. Then, while Brittany was the cradle of Post-Impressionist painting, Normandy was one of the fountainheads of Impressionism and its precursor, French naturalistic landscape painting. Moreover, Normandy, besides yielding one of the most important schools of French Romanesque and Gothic architecture has one of the most attractive vernacular building styles in Europe, with much of its architectural heritage sensitively restored following war damage.

Normandy holds a special place in the development of British and French landscape painting and even today, despite the development of industry around its ports and cities, Normandy remains essentially rural. The skies, the light, the cliffs and the beaches of its coastline, especially that between Dieppe and Etretat and along the Normandy Corniche, at Deauville, Trouville and Honfleur, cast their spell over French artists just as the East Anglian landscape did over John Constable, Thomas Gainsborough and the Norwich School of painters. In the same way the valley of the Seine, with its abbeys and castles and its great city of Rouen, held an enduring fascination for both English and French artists.

After Waterloo

The English were quick to discover Normandy after Waterloo, and among the earliest visitors were the Norwich School artists, John Berney Crome and George Vincent, who 'belched as loud as the steam packet' on the rough crossing from England, with John Sell Cotman and Henry Edridge following in 1817, the latter being among the first to record the picturesque scenes for the new type of English tourist. By the 1820s a host of English artists including J.M.W. Turner, Richard Parkes Bonington and Samuel Prout had begun to exploit the country's architectural and landscape riches. Bonington, besides travelling throughout Normandy in 1821 with the French artist Alexandre Colin, became a friend of Paul Huet, the French landscape painter who, with Eugène Boudin, anticipated many of the innovations of Impressionist painting. Huet's oil and watercolour landscape sketches, influenced by Bonington and Constable, were painted during many visits to Normandy.

Boudin, born in Honfleur in 1824 and called by his friend J.B. Corot 'Master of the Skies', spent his life in Le Havre where he taught the young Claude Monet, framed pictures for the painters Thomas Couture and J.F. Millet, and painted brilliant out-door sketches of the beaches at Trouville and Deauville. In 1865 Monet worked with Gustave Courbet at Trouville but his colour reached its highest pitch in paintings of the Alabaster Coast between Etretat and Dieppe, the tall cliffs of Etretat itself and the wild scenery around Varengeville-sur-mer, where he painted the church and the cemetery, resting place of the father of Cubism, Georges Braque. Monet lived and worked also in the Seine Valley, painting at Rouen his great series of the cathedral façade, sometimes called the Sistine Chapel of Impressionism. He settled finally on the eastern border of Normandy, at Giverny, and created his celebrated watergarden which remains a popular attraction.

Honfleur and Dieppe drew painters who were to break through the frontiers of Impressionism. In his series of seascapes painted at Honfleur in the summer of 1886, Georges Seurat echoed the classical spirit of perhaps the greatest Norman artist of all, Nicolas Poussin. But it was Dieppe that became Normandy's equivalent of Brittany's Pont-Aven and, for a century, the haunt of numerous artists, English and French. At the start, as Benjamin Robert Haydon wrote in 1814, Dieppe was 'dark, old, snuffy and picturesque' and, in the 1850s, Eugène Delacroix could lie gloomily in bed watching the masts of ships in the harbour and loathe the new English steamers for their 'mean form'. By the 1880s, however, Dieppe was a relatively salubrious haven of fashionable French and English society with the Prime Minister, Lord Salisbury, enjoying a family retreat at nearby Puys and the Prince of Wales, later Edward VII, making fleeting incognito visits to the area, while artists and writers added to the general entertainment. The studio of Jacques Emile Blanche, decorated by his friend, Pierre Auguste Renoir, became a rendezvous for Monet, Walter Sickert, the ageing Camille Pissarro and, in the 1890s, the thin, dying figure of Aubrey Beardsley, who spent his last summer in a pension rented earlier by James Whistler. The improving ambience of Dieppe, the elegant decadence of its casino in contrast with the filthy alleys of Le Pollet, fascinated the English artist, Sickert, who painted the scene secretly in his studio before moving in with a fishwife. In 1895 Charles Conder, the

Australian painter, came with Henry Harland, editor of the famous *Yellow Books*, while the turn of the century saw Dieppe in its social heyday, glittering with famous writers and musicians as well as painters. The Café des Tribunaux, which still exists, was the favourite rendezvous for smart talk and parties.

Rouen's Treasures

Normandy has some major public collections of French painting, the most important centred in Rouen and Caen, with specialist collections in Dieppe, Cherbourg, Honfleur and Le Havre, and with small but good collections elsewhere, such as Alençon, Coutances and Trouville. Rouen is a truly romantic city offering such a surfeit of visual pleasure that the visitor is wise to take it in small doses, and its Musée des Beaux Arts, as Normandy's Louvre, should be viewed selectively to avoid aching feet and a spinning head.

Established at the end of the Revolution, in 1804, Rouen's collections were housed first in the Abbey of St Ouen and then, in 1887, rehoused in one of those fatiguing monumental museum buildings that sprang up all over Europe in the 19th century. The museum has lofty ceilings, stone floors and an institutional atmosphere, but the collection is one of the richest in France, containing Flemish, Dutch, Italian, Spanish and French works from the 16th to the 20th centuries. It stands in Rue Thiers with the entrance on Place Verdrel.

A rewarding first visit might take in the room of portraits by Blanche of his Anglo-French artistic circle in Dieppe, including Jean Cocteau and André Gide; the gallery devoted to the great Romantic painter Théodore Géricault, born in Rouen in 1791; and the enjoyable collection of Impressionist painting. Lovers of classical painting might then return to study the French School: magnificent *Diana in her Bath*, now firmly attributed to François Clouet, two superb works by Nicolas Poussin, born at Les Andelys in 1593; and a fine painting of the *Dream of Polyphile* by a follower of Poussin and pupil of Simon Vouet, Eustache Le Sueur. Then there are three masterpieces of French 19th-century painting: Géricault's famous *Officier des Carabiniers*, Eugène Delacroix's enormous and celebrated *Justice of Trajan* and the delicious small portrait of *La Belle Zélie* (Madame Aymon), painted by J.A. Ingres in 1806.

There are some masterpieces from the Flemish school: Gérard David's *Virgin and Saints*, including a powerful self portrait; Martin de Vos' *Elijah and Rebecca*; Peter Paul Rubens' *Adoration of the Shepherds*; and a deeply moving portrait of a young woman on her death bed by an unknown Flemish artist of the 17th century. The Italian *chef d'oeuvres* are Perugino's magnificent predella, from an altar piece, showing the Adoration, Baptism and Resurrection; Paolo Veronese's *St Barnaby Healing a Sick Man*; and Caravaggio's *Flagellation of Christ*. And as well as these collections Rouen has superb applied art, including the famous Rouen *faïence* (tin-glazed earthenware), which reached its heyday in the 18th century before the import of English wares ruined the French trade.

Apart from the sheer beauty of Rouen's situation in the valley of the Seine, cloaked by hills and lush woods, its ecclesiastic and secular buildings have long made it a place of architectural pilgrimage. When Cotman visited Rouen in 1818 he said there were enough subjects there and in the immediate vicinity to occupy him for a fortnight. The view of the city from Mount Ste Catherine, with its landmarks, remains magnificent: the cathedral, the great churches of St Maclou and St Ouen, the splendid Palais de Justice, the narrow streets of timber-framed medieval houses: all these provided Cotman, and other artists, with a mass of material. And, thanks to painstaking restoration and conservation, the old quarter of Rouen is still much as it appeared to a Norwich newspaper editor, Seth Stevenson, in 1816, 'a scene, in which the useful woorkes of modern industry were so intimately blended with the imposing remains and majestic monuments of ancient power and ancient faith'.

The cathedral, built over four centuries, with its great tower and spire, replaced in cast iron after being burned down in 1822, almost defeated Cotman: 'How to finish it? what a thing it is!' A masterpiece of Flamboyant Gothic style, the cathedral overwhelms with its richness; while the abbey church of St Ouen, in the Place Général de Gaulle, although easier to digest, is no less beautiful, especially its coronetted central tower. The same style is brilliantly expressed also in the church of St Maclou, now being restored after war damage. The builders in the late Gothic style soon adopted the ornate Renaissance motifs introduced to Normandy after the French kings began invading Italy in 1494 and Rouen's Palais de Justice, attributed to Roulland le Roux and now much restored, is an outstanding Norman example of the new style, as is the famous Gros Horloge, the most often painted building in Rouen.

Art in Caen

Caen, while affecting a more modern and easygoing ambience, is almost as rich as Rouen in historical and artistic interest. Severely damaged in World War II, the city centre was almost eliminated, but prominent historic buildings, including the Abbayes aux Hommes and aux Dames, the churches of St Pierre and St Sauveur and the castle, were saved. Caen university has a centre for medieval archaeological research which bases much of its work on the interesting material housed by the Musée de Normandie situated within the castle walls; and this museum contains also important collections relating to the social and historical development of Normandy.

Within the castle precinct is the Musée des Beaux Arts, smaller than that at Rouen, but including major works. This collection, formed in 1793, was quite substantial by the time the museum was inaugurated officially in 1801. The original building was destroyed in the war, the collections being evacuated for safety until the present museum could re-open in 1970. The gallery is light, simply furnished in neutral colours, with small rooms that allow pictures to be seen in comfort; and each room has a short guide singling out major works. The Mancel collection contains some 3,000 works as well as some 50,000 Flemish, Dutch, German, English, French and Italian prints, including a number by Rubens, Rembrandt van Rijn and Albrecht Durer. A fine group of 17th- and 18th-century works is displayed in small rooms with leaded windows, carpets and furniture, creating a 'domestic' setting; and in this collection there are outstanding Dutch paintings by Saloman Ruysdael, Jan van Goyen and Adriaen van Ostade, as well as Limoges enamels and miniatures. The Mancel collection also has early masterpieces housed in the main galleries: a *Virgin and Child* by Roger van der Weyden, *St Jacques* by Cosimo Tura, the superb *Marriage of the Virgin* by Perugino and an outstanding piece of ivory sculpture, a *Virgin and Child*, of the 13th-century French School.

The main collection ranges from the 16th to the close of the 19th century and the masterpieces include: (from the 16th century) Paris Bordone's *Annunciation*, Jacopo Tintoretto's *Descent from the Cross* and Paolo Veronese's *Temptation of St Anthony*; (from the 17th century) Luca Giordano's *Rape of Helen*, Poussin's *Death of Adonis*, Rubens' *Abraham and Melchissedech*, the *Conversion of St Augustin* by Gerard de Lairesse, the *Samaritan* by Philippe de Champaigne; (from the 18th century) a lovely portrait by Hyacinthe Rigaud, a delicious François Boucher pastoral, works by J.B. Pater and the Rouen-born artist Jean Restout. There are also some good 19th-century French works such as Pierre Narcisse Guerin's *Bonaparte at Cairo*, Géricault's *Course de Cheval* and several small paintings by Delacroix, Couture and the Barbizon landscape artsists Théodore Rousseau, Jules Dupré and C.F. Daubigny. There is also a small group of 20th-century Impressionist and Post-Impressionist works.

Caen has spared no effort in restoring and renewing its war-damaged districts. William the Conqueror's castle keep and the barbicans of the two main gates still have parts of the 12th-century fabric. The Flamboyant Gothic and Renaissance churches of St Pierre and St Sauveur (formally Notre Dame de Froide-Rue) are looking quite good, although the exterior fabric of soft Caen limestone suffers continuing erosion. And there are some fine 18th-century houses at Place St Sauveur, which features a comic statue of Louis XIV as a Roman emperor. But Caen's greatest survival is the Abbaye aux Hommes which, with the church of St Etienne and its separate sister house, the Abbaye aux Dames, was built originally by the Conqueror and his Queen Matilda, to be largely rebuilt in the 18th century and restored extensively in the recent post-war years. The contents include outstanding 18th-century rooms and staircases, a 14th-century guard room, now the city's council chamber, paintings by the 17th- and 18th-century artists Pierre Mignard, Sébastien Bourdon, Michel Lépicié and Jean Restout, and St Etienne church has one of the most austerely beautiful Romanesque façades in Normandy.

Caen, in retaining the best of its past, has not hesitated to build anew, in a traditional French style, along widened streets with opened vistas; and with some exceptions, including the station square, the general effect is impressive.

Norman Architecture

The Normandy architectural landscape is an intriguing mixture of what is at once strange and familiar to the British eye. The Renaissance chateaux, the long, low timber-framed farmhouses and barns, the stocky yellow country churches with their black witches' steeples, are unmistakably Norman. But the fat towers, the square donjons of Normandy castles, the severe purity of its abbeys, their round-headed arches, arcading, chevron, zig-zag, billet and key patterns, remind us of our indissoluble Anglo-Norman heritage.

After the conquest the Norman builders in England created

the Benedictine churches, cathedrals and abbeys at Durham, Canterbury, Norwich and Westminster, all larger than their sister buildings in Normandy and with Western towers. The St Etienne church in Caen with its Romanesque façade was influential in the spread of the style in both Normandy and England, and is matched only by the purity of Jumièges consecrated ten years before, in 1067, although other fine Romanesque buildings survive in part, including those at Bayeux, Crueilly and St Martin de Boscherville.

At Bayeux, famous for its 11th-century tapestry, the early cathedral suffered at the hands of the English, and little remains of the Romanesque building except the splendidly solid base of the nave and the two towers of the façade, to which spires were added in the 13th century. Today, fine as it is as an example of Norman Gothic, Bayeux's cathedral has to yield precedence to the massive one at Coutances, also rebuilt following destruction in 1218, its position on a hill emphasising its soaring lines unimpeded by ornamentation of the piers.

Normandy Gothic architecture of the 13th century has marked characteristics such as square towers with tall belfry lights crowned with spires, high lancet windows and rich mouldings. The tower of St Pierre at Caen is the finest example with its elaborate parapet, open work pinnacles and lofty belfry lights, but the great lantern tower of Coutances has been called the 'finest thing of its kind in France'; while the wealth of mouldings of Rouen cathedral and the church of St Maclou show the influence of rich English Foliage sculpture.

The south porch of the church of Notre Dame at Louviers is perhaps the most elaborate Flamboyant design in existence, and it certainly attracted English artists in the 1820s and 1830s. The churches of St Pierre and St Sauveur in Caen both adapted Renaissance detail to Gothic plans but secular buildings such as Rouen's Palais de Justice and Gros Horloge were the most extreme expression of the style.

Vernacular Normandy houses and barns can be seen at the

recently opened Musée Schlumberger at Crèvecoeur-en-Auge. With plentiful supplies of wood making it the principal domestic building material, the shipbuilder Jean Ango of Dieppe built an entire palace in wood in the 16th century. This was destroyed by the British in the following century but the church of Ste Catherine at Honfleur, built of wood, still survives.

The numerous timber-framed houses of Rouen, exposed through extensive restoration, speak for themselves while proving how the style has persisted through to this century. Virtually the whole of the smart, modern seaside resort of Deauville, including many large summer villas built in the 1940s and 1950s, is created in this *style normand classique.* In sharp contrast, however, are the extensive acres of concrete blocks that make up Le Havre today: apart from this truly dramatic aberration and the regrettable ugliness of rebuilt Cherbourg, it is the prevailing sensitive awareness of the heritage of unity between urban and rural that makes Normandy such a pleasing and often stunning visual experience.

* * * *

In Honfleur, along the road from Deauville to Le Havre, the most remarkable feature is not really the quay, which seems disappointingly grey and shabby, but that curious all wood 15th- to 16th-century church of Ste Catherine with its separate belfry. Built by ships' carpenters, it is a rare West European survival with some magnificent 16th-century carving, especially that of the musicians along the gallery and of the angels on the roof arcading. There is also a statue of St Etienne, patron saint of the 14th-century church in the Vieux Bassin, which now houses the maritime museum.

Apart from the exquisite 17th-century chapel of Notre Dame de Grace on the hillside above the town, the other major interest in Honfleur is the Musée Boudin situated off Rue de L'Homme de Bois in Place Erik Satie. Enlarged in 1972, this now includes an extension commemorating Honfleur's greatest glory, Eugène Boudin. This room, flooded with light from a window-wall overlooking the Seine, also houses works by the landscape painters Huet, Daubigny, Georges Michel and J.B. Isabey, although the effect is marred somewhat by a sculpture of silly wooden geese by Raymond Bigot. The museum also has 19th-century works by Xavier Le Prince, born in Honfleur in 1799, and Charles Mozin, and the top floor houses 20th-century paintings by Raoul Dufy, Monet, Paul Signac, an absurd large picture of cows by Adolphe Marais and one surprise, a painting of Honfleur by Amédée Oxenfant.

Modern Le Havre

Classical rationalism was the guiding spirit of Normandy's rebuilding of war-devastated Le Havre, and this great seaport today is important to anyone with more than a passing interest in the planned development of a modern city. Le Havre is a monument to Auguste Perret, one of the fathers of modern architecture, a teacher of Le Corbusier and the man who, according to Reyner Banham, 'more than any other made reinforced concrete acceptable as a visible building material'. Perret's fluted concrete columns, beams and panels, his clearly articulated structures are a legacy to the work of younger architects world-wide.

The old town of Le Havre, built by the Siennese architect, Gerolamo Bellamarti in 1541, was the first example in France of large-scale urban planning. Four centuries later the town again opted for the gridiron system in adopting the model reconstruction proposed by Perret based on the classical scheme of straight lines and wide perspectives, although Perret's more radical idea of elevating the roads above the town was rejected. At first sight the town seems strangely unFrench, lacking as it does the untidiness and comfortable intimacy of Dieppe or Calais. But a walk from the station to the main square, Place de L'Hôtel de Ville, reveals some surviving examples of French Art Deco architecture, such as the Egyptian motifs of the Ecole Pratique de Commerce et d'Industrie de Jeunes Filles, and these survivals throwing into even sharper relief the monumental block of the Town Hall, centre piece of Perret's entire scheme, which, with its severe, almost Germanic façade declares the autocratic quality of his design.

To the west is Perret's oddly awe-inspiring *pièce de resistance*, the church of St Joseph, overwhelmingly secular in its appeal, a kind of fantastic filmset from *Star Wars*, the tower with its pyramidal base sitting like an alien spacecraft in a treeless square. Through the gaping entrance hatch the interior shocks by its geometric severity, with the huge concrete piers supporting an octagonal lantern relieved by squares and oblongs of stained glass, while the central altar, enclosed by a kind of *baldiccino* canopy, gives the feeling more of a lecture hall than a place of worship.

After St Joseph the André Malraux Fine Arts Museum (Chaussée John Kennedy), built of glass and metal with high windows facing the sea, seems reassuringly familiar. It has as a sentinel a huge bronze-finished sculpture by Henri-Georges Adam by whom there is a similar, smaller piece called *La Flèche* in Rouen's museum. Le Havre's museum is famed for its collections of over 200 paintings and 70 drawings by Boudin, and of paintings by Raoul Dufy, the Fauvist, who was born in Le Havre.

The collection also contains 100 or so works by important 19th- and 20th-century French artists, including Michel, Géricault, Delacroix, J.B. Corot and Henri Fantin-Latour. The Boudins are a pleasure to the eye, displayed in a way that shows clearly the artist's development from his naturalistic work of the 1850s, such as the almost Dutch-like *Pardon de Sainte Anne la Palud*, completed in 1858, to his exquisite later oil and gouache sketches of the seaward sky and his brilliantly coloured figures painted out of doors on the Trouville and Deauville beaches.

Before leaving Normandy, among the lesser collections worth mentioning are the pleasant Dieppe museum, in a castle high above the esplanade, with its unique collection of ivories dating from the middle ages, prints by Braque and paintings of local scenes; and the Musée Thomas Henry, now housed in Cherbourg's new arts centre, including works by the locally-born Millet, whose toiling peasants imprint themselves on the memory.

Besides Normandy

While Normandy is the most rewarding destination for art lovers, the provinces on either side are not to be dismissed. To the west, in Brittany, there are good museums at Rennes, Quimper and Brest, the last two being of particular interest for their collection of works from the Pont-Aven school. The rocky coastlines and fishing communities, particularly of the west coast, are associated irrevocably with the great 19th-century painters who followed on after the Impressionists, especially Paul Gauguin and his circle. Gauguin's friend, Emile Bernard, is well represented and in Brest there is the lesser-known Georges Lacombe.

The fine museum at Rennes which is housed in old university buildings on Quai Emile Zola, has some good 19th-century works including a Gauguin. The collection's strength lies, however, in its diversity ranging from 16th-century Dutch to present day local painters with the main emphasis on the French School. Georges de Latour's *The New Born (Le Nouveau Né)* is considered the master piece, while a selection from the substantial holding of drawings is always on display.

To the east of Normandy, Pas de Calais is not so often associated with artists, but as soon as Napoleon was finally defeated a wave of English watercolour painters set to work, as photographers might today, to depict, for sale to their fellow-countrymen, now crossing the Channel in ever greater numbers, harbour scenes and other familiar land falls in this nearest part of France, as well as some of the picturesque inland towns such as St Omer, Abbeville, Beauvais and Amiens.

By a happy chance a Frenchman, François Louis Francia, who had painted for some 20 years in England, returned to live in his native Calais in 1816 and became a natural focal point. Perhaps Francia's greatest contribution was to give lessons to the teenage Bonington, whose father had just transferred his lace-making manufactory from Nottingham. Amazingly precocious, Bonington who was to die of consumption at the age of only 25, became a rare link between the English and French schools, owing as much to his Paris friends and contemporaries, Delacroix, Isabey, Huet and Colin, as to his English background. His first success was in the Paris Salon of 1821 where he was recognised as bringing a breath of fresh air to studio-bound French art. The influence of Bonington, reinforced by Constable whose pictures were soon also to be appreciated in the Salon, helped prompt the growth of naturalistic painting in France with Boudin, Corot, Daubigny, Stanislas Lépine and Rousseau paving the way for Monet, Sisley and their friends.

Boulogne's small, friendly museum, besides Napoleonic relics and some interesting ceramics, has paintings by Boucher, Corot and Sisley; while Calais has its grander, well presented Musée des Beaux Arts et de la Dentelle with paintings from the European Schools, sculptures by Rodin and Bourtelle, and a room devoted to the history of lace-making. The former occupies an inconspicuous town house and the latter an imposing modern edifice, these being exceptions to the rule that, in this north-east corner of France, the public museums are often notable, not only for their contents, but for the historic interest and distinction of the buildings which house them. Thus, in Amiens there is the fine, late 19th-century Musée de Picardie with its staircase dominated by Puvis de Chavanne's splendid murals. The bold decorative quality of his work, of which there is also an example in Rouen, was much admired by Gauguin and Vincent van

Gogh. An unusual feature of this collection is the primitive 16th-century works of the Confrèrie du Puy Notre Dame d'Amiens and one gallery is devoted to 19th- and 20th-century local artists who include Francis Tattegrain, a prize-winning painter whose dramatic works are to be found in nearly all the northern museums. If the intriguing self-portrait of the famous pastellist, Quentin de la Tour, whets the appetite, it may be recalled that his home town of St Quentin is not far away, and the Musée Antoine Lécuyer in that town celebrates the work of this painter of French 18th-century high society. His contemporaries, who include J.B. Chardin and J.H. Fragonard are well represented in Amiens and, among the later French works there, is a fine view of Mont Saint-Michel by J.B. Isabey.

The Musée des Beaux Arts at Arras, housed in the beautiful old abbey St Vaast, is one of the most pleasurable to visit thanks also to its obliging staff. In the refectory there is a relief plan of the town in the 18th century. It was near here that Corot later found inspiration for some of his finest work, and he and his followers are a feature of the museum, with Henri-Joseph Dutilleux's paintings often mistaken for Corot's, their gentle charm lulling the critical eye. The grand cloister is reserved for temporary exhibitions but on permanent display you will find early French and Flemish art, sculptures in wood and porcelain from Arras and Tournai.

In Douai the museum is in the exquisite old charterhouse, Rue des Chartreux, and, besides displays of the city as it was in the 18th century, there are collections of Roman and medieval findings, some 16th-century paintings from the Low Countries, including *A Battle in a Village* by the younger Breughel, a fine *Flagellation of Christ* by Ludovico Carracci, and some enjoyable works by the Impressionists.

Valenciennes is especially proud of its connection with the arts. Its tradition of good sculptors ranges from the 14th-century André Beauneveu to Jean-Baptiste Carpeaux, best known for his controversial *Dance Group* designed for the Opera in Paris and completed in 1866. A gallery in Valencienne's spacious Musée des Beaux Arts is dedicated to Carpeaux's work and there is a splendid portrait of another local sculptor, *Antoine Pater*, by the greatest Valenciennois, J.A. Watteau. Watteau's pupil, J.B. Pater, is also represented by two charming scenes; and there are good paintings from the 17th-century Flemish School, including Rubens' *Rainbow*.

The Lille Collection

France, lacking Britain's infinite variety of country houses open to the public, relies more heavily on its institutions for displays of culture, with benefit to the towns and cities that play host to the main collections. Lille, is much enhanced by its outstanding Palais des Beaux Arts (Place de la République) built in the late 19th century to replace the original museum initiated by Napoleon. The collection owes its particular interest to Edouard Reynard, curator in the middle years of the last century, whose policy was to acquire sketches as well as major paintings. Thus, a huge Rubens *Crucifixion* is accompanied by an oil sketch of the same subject; and Delacroix's magnificent *Médée* by a wonderfully free small study which gives an insight into the character of the artist. Louis Léopold Boilly, born in nearby La Bassée, is best known for his *Studio of Isabey*, which is in the Louvre, but Lille has his oil studies of the artists depicted in this masterpiece as well as a major painting, the *Triumph of Marat*, which marked a turning point in Boilly's career, ingratiating him with the revolutionary elements which had threatened his life. His great Neo-classical contemporary, Jacques Louis David, is represented by an important early work, *Belisarius Asking Alms*, and by the *Emperor Napoleon*, the latter remaining in the memory as a truly powerful picture by the greatest exponent of Neo-classicism.

David's friend, J.J. Wicar, who worked in Rome, bequeathed

his own collection of drawings and works of art to Lille and the gift, which includes Donatello's *Feast of Herod* as well as numerous drawings by Raphael, Michelangelo and Poussin, is one of the features of the museum. Apart from this, of particular note are the 15th-century Dutch masterpiece by Dierik Bouts, *The Earthly Paradise* and, in the next century, *The Haycart* by Jan Sieberechts, one of the first painters of English landscape. A whole room is given to Jacob Jordaens as well as one to his master, Rubens. The Spanish School has a fine El Greco, *St Francis at Prayer*, and contrasting pictures by Goya y Lucientes, one of hideous old age, the other of youthful charm. There is a strong representation of French portraits including Paul Robert's modern-looking *Woman* painted at Rome in 1722, a typical early 18th-century work by Nicolas de Largillière and Renoir's *Young Lady in a Black Hat.* Outstanding is another Impressionist painting, *The Seine at the Bridge of Suresnes*, a study of light on water, and compared with the almost Dutch looking *The Seine at Villeneuve St Georges*, painted 22 years earlier by Théodore Rousseau, shows the development of French painting in this period.

For the best single collection in this region Lille, which considers itself second only to the Louvre, is probably the one to sample, with Rouen and Rennes as close seconds. Lille has the extra advantage of being within easy reach of the good museums at Arras, Douai and Valenciennes, and not far from Amiens, where the outstanding cathedral is an additional magnet. In these parts francophiles may savour not only the power and professionalism of traditional French art, which in grandeur dwarfed anything from across the Channel, the history paintings alone astounding or depressing by their very magnitude; but they may savour also that particular French genius, the more remarkable for its emergence in the mid-19th century from a strictly academic background, to blossom and flower so abundantly with the Impressionists. And this art, with all the gaiety and light associated with southern shores, was based firmly just across the water from England: thus the Briton, by seeing northern France through their eyes, can help to open his own, much of what they painted being still there, on his doorstep, to be enjoyed today.

Chapter 9 : Food, Drink, Presents and Pastimes

Fresh chilled orange juice, buttery *croissants*, crisp French bread, coffee as only France seems to know how to make it: what more appetising start to your first morning on the other side of the Channel? And the temptation follows you everywhere, one of the most exotic smells of France being that of the boulangerie, patisserie and *salon de thé* in any shopping street. Since the Gaulloise went out of favour it is the characteristic aroma from these shops which makes France such a mouthwatering country.

French Menus

However, at the mundane everyday level of eating main meals, particularly in the towns, it must be said that French fare is often no better than British, though exceptions will be found, not least in the smaller, patron-run place. In the snack area, we have the growing menace of the *croque monsieur*, a fast-toasted, processed-cheese sandwich with a thin layer of packaged ham, not really in the same class as a Welsh rarebit. And what are we to make of gastronomic artistry when we find more and more emphasis on such standbys as *crêpes* and *tartes aux pommes*, not to mention that awful ubiquitous entrail-filled sausage known as *andouillette*?

Apart from the large and pricey *grande cuisine* establishments, you would do well to follow any French bourgeois family in earnest pursuit of a best buy. But hurry, for where these cognoscenti settle there will be no room left for the unbooked stranger within half-an-hour of opening time. If there is no one around to follow, study the menus on display after taking advice from a discerning restaurant guide, like the Red Michelin with its clear indication of prices and, where rosettes are awarded, a note of culinary specialities.

I refer so far to the moderately or lower priced set menus, to *les menus touristiques*, and at this level of eating out in northern France be prepared for a lack of vitamin C, of fruits, salads and vegetables; and with the cooking butter rather than oil based and the spread everywhere of *frites*, often a too closely related cousin of the worst of British chips, the hungry visitor may before long suffer both increase in girth and constipation.

Much fuss is made in those parts of seafoods, no doubt with justification; and certainly the crustacean fan in single-minded search for lobster, crab, prawn and oyster will not be disappointed. But, if fresh, these creatures, surely, taste much the same everywhere, the accompanying sauces making the difference and the French approach to mayonnaise and herby butter or garlicky sauces has much to commend it compared with the tendency in England to weigh them down with flour.

And meat: beautiful tender veal served as *escalope*, whether simply or with delectable sauces: nowadays, as in England, it is more likely to be pork or chicken; and when it comes to red meat, why cross the Channel? But, for spicey and aromatic concoctions such as soups, daubes, stews, in which undoubtedly the French excel; for *hors d'oeuvres*, omelettes, salads and cheeses: if you are looking for tasty, inexpensive bargains of *that* ilk then, yes, only France will do.

* * * *

These strictures apply more to Nord/Pas de Calais and Brittany than to Normandy where the catering traditions are, on the one hand, more distinctively regional and, on the other, more cosmopolitan, more exposed to sophisticated palates from further afield. In any case, the truth is that, when we say we enjoyed a meal in France, it is usually not only of the food and wine that we speak. In France, above all countries, it is the total experience that counts: *le patron*'s flair and devotion to his craft; the prompt, competent, professional service by clean, well-mannered waiters; the bustling air and sense of occasion; an ambience which permits on the one hand a sense of privacy, a feeling of being inconspicuous, and on the other close identification with the world at large: with passers-by in the street, which always seems to be part of the scene, with the energy given off by the eager chat in which one's neighbours indulge, regardless of their class or sex. And if one is travelling alone, particularly if female, one can be quite happy in a French café, brasserie or restaurant in a way in which one cannot feel at ease alone in the English equivalent.

Traditional Dishes

Some of the traditional dishes and delicacies of the region will no doubt be of interest to most visitors to northern France. In Nord/Pas de Calais and Picardy, soups are important, with *soupe des hortilllons* perhaps the best known, being made from the vegetables for which the area is famous, cauliflowers from St Omer and carrots from St Valéry, to name but two. Apart from *andouillettes*, usually associated with Arras, the duck paté in pastry of Amiens is a highlight. *La ficelle picarde* is a ham pancake with a mushroom sauce, and rissoles may be filled with fish or meat and served with a thick sauce. Seafood specialities include sole, turbot, fresh and smoked herring with cream, shrimps, mussels, fish shops sometimes doubling as restaurants. Macaroons are a feature of southern Picardy, while Lille offers a wide choice of delectable confectionery and patisserie, much of it from shop counters opening on to the street.

Flemish cuisine relies heavily on casseroles, often flavoured with beer. Local cheeses are for the most part very strong. One, *Vieux Puant*, known more politely as *Vieux Lille*, is forbidden by bye-law to be carried in a taxi. Other types include Maroilles, even stronger, *Bergues, Rollot* and, a mild variety, *Mont des Cats*.

According to the Green Michelin, 'Breton cooking is characterised more by quality of the materials used than by fine preparation'. Seafoods are excellent, the most famous dish probably being lobster *à l'Armoricaine*, while *Cotriade* is a Breton equivalent of *bouillabaisse* fish soup. The mutton is good, served often with white beans, and Morlaix produces a particularly good ham. Vegetables of local note include potatoes, artichokes, cauliflowers and peas. Breton *crêpes* and *galettes* are kinds of pancake served alone or with sweet or savoury fillings; and confectionery includes *praline* made at Rennes.

Much of Norman cookery is based on butter, cream and, if not wine, cider or calvados. Rouen offers succulent duck, Caen is famous for tripe while there are various treatments of sole, *Dieppois* being perhaps the best known. Food from the Pays d'Auge, an area famous for its chicken, is often cooked with apples and/or small onions. Notable among the cheeses are *Pont-l'Evêque*, the stronger *Livarot* and the famous *Camembert*. Finally, with so many apples around, there are *tartes aux pommes* everywhere.

As for drink, the wine connoisseur will be disappointed. Apart from the widely available Muscadet, this is beer and cider country, with nearly a quarter of all French beer brewed in Nord/Pas de Calais. Calvados and Benedictine are the two leading liqueurs. Since the best apples are grown in Calvados, Normandy ought to be the best place to drink cider but, surprisingly, this is not well exploited, the pale *cidre bouché* being often the only version available to the customer.

Food on Ferries

As one tends to eat one's way across the Channel as well as on the other side, a word about food on board the car ferries may not be amiss. In a few cases, a rough sea enabling one to start again after throwing up afloat can be a blessing, but by and large the victuals dished out to passengers at sea are well up to the British norm if rather short of the French. I have heard it said that where, as with some Sealink services, you can choose between a British and French ship, the latter is usually the better bet for both its service and its food, but I am not so sure.

As I have seen them, whatever the vessel's nationality, restaurant, cafeteria and bar services on most cross-Channel ferries tend to be on a perfunctory take-it-or-leave-it basis. If any firm is to set a good example, it ought to be the all-French Brittany Ferries. I found the facilities inviting but opening hours limited, not always in tune with the needs of the passengers' stomachs. Then, when I sought lunch in the *Prince of Brittany's* attractive restaurant a cashier demanded payment in advance for a meal the ingredients of which were neither visible to me, in kind or in writing, nor known to her. The head steward, being summoned, tried to brush me off but I insisted on some description of the dishes before paying my money. After that, I may add, it was all smiles from the staff who do appreciate *some* sign of interest.

As for the menu, when eventually I got dug into it: for 60F, four courses plus quarter bottle of wine, the main event being a choice between veal cutlets, chicken stew, spicey sausages and cold meats with salad, all looking very appetising and tasting very bland.

Well, as I said, the food is not everything.

Shopping

When shopping for food it is important to remember that, with the exceptions of cheeses, packaged or in their original farmhouse state, *charcuterie* and some *vins de table*, food shopping in France does not necessarily save the British great sums of money. Much of the pleasure and satisfaction lies in the mouth-watering way the produce is displayed, the appetising packaging of even the most banal convenience foods and the wide choice on offer, not least of tempting pre-cooked dishes usually unavailable in England. Among these you will find, as first courses, *quiches* made with cream; *celeriac à la remoulade*; Russian salad in real mayonnaise; leeks in lemon and oil; tomatoes filled with shrimps and mayonnaise; stuffed courgettes and peppers, and various locally made *patés* and *terrines* including *rillettes* of pork, a Breton speciality. As second courses you will find cold beef in jelly (*boeuf à la mode*); chicken pancakes; and slices of veal in a tuna and caper flavoured mayonnaise. As last courses, you will find a stunning range of *patisseries, tartes, gateaux* and, not least, *croissants*. There are also several bottled sauces, and some canned vegetables, notably *petits pois*, and a few packet soups, not least fish soups, that may be good buys.

* * * *

Clothing at the higher end of the market is certainly as expensive, if not more so, than similar garments in Britain, although once again the variety can be greater, particularly in the wealthier towns. The big, popular department stores to be found in most of the larger places, such as Monoprix and Prisunic, sell excellent, very cheap children's clothes, but those of other well-known designers are often at the Harrod's price level.

Lace from Calais and, perhaps, pottery from Dinan are worth considering. Whatever the milieu, the serious shopper is generally treated with care and respect not often accorded him or her in England. So, if you are not prepared to look carefully before you buy, to give shopping the time and serious consideration that the *vendor* thinks it deserves, you have only yourself to blame if you find yourself fobbed off with a poor bargain. Otherwise, the rule, generally, should be: 'If you like it, buy it, but don't assume you couldn't buy it just as well at home.'

Sporting Activities

With a climate much the same as southern England's, what you get up to out of doors in northern France will depend usually on the weather. But the choice is enormous. Not only does the long coastline offer a wide variety of salt-water pursuits, but there is a good deal of sheltered water in the rivers and canals of the region. CRUISING has long been popular over there, and most ports and harbours, coastal and estuarial, provide first-class yacht berthing and chandling facilities. On the coast, water-skiing, sailing, windsurfing and sand-yachting are widely available. Le Touquet, with its enormous sandy beach, is one of the best bases for these sports. In Brittany alone, there are over 150 sailing schools. Useful bases for snorkelling and skin-diving include Trebeurden, Cherbourg and Le Havre.

And then, besides DINGHY SAILING, BOATING and BARGING on estuaries, canals or rivers, there is CANOEING, a popular pastime throughout the region. The rivers present easy to intermediate conditions, although the advanced canoeist will find plenty to tax him on, for example, the Gouet and the Sarre. There are forty clubs in Brittany, and in Normandy, Caen is a good base. Further east, Boulogne, St Omer and Berck, among others, provide opportunities.

SEA FISHING is free and no authorisation is needed so long as regulations concerning catch quotas, military zones, port controls and effluent disposal are complied with. The nearest tourist office can indicate which local restrictions are in force. FRESH-WATER FISHING is rather different. A fishing tax may be payable, and it is usually necessary to belong to one of the 4,056 French angling associations, many of which have reciprocal arrangements with British clubs. Temporary membership is often obtainable locally through fishing tackle shops and riverside restaurants or hotels. For the dedicated angler, the Aulne in western Brittany offers particularly good salmon fishing, while further east the Somme, Authie and Canche all provide excellent sport, the Authie being especially rich in trout.

RIDING is available almost everywhere, often with marked circuits covering large distances, sometimes with suitable accommodation en route. In Nord/Pas de Calais alone there are 1,500 kilometres of route specially recorded on maps, and these come under the same auspices as those for walkers, cyclists and canoeists: the Fédération Régionale des Associations de Randonnée, the French equivalent of the Rambler's Association. Horse-drawn carriages may be hired in Brittany, Picardy and Normandy, and horse-racing devotees will be happiest at Le Touquet and Deauville. In late August, the latter holds its world-famous Grand Prix, one of the most important prizes in the French racing calendar. CYCLING, too, is an important French sport, and immensely popular. It is possible to hire bicycles almost everywhere, from the rail station, a youth hostel or the local tourist office.

Normandy has more GOLF courses than the other provinces covered by this book: with nine on the coast alone, an enthusiast's family can be left happily on the beach while the fanatics are at play. Nord/Pas de Calais and Picardy are also well endowed, and Brittany has several. As for green fees, there is often a higher rate at weekends and several clubs offer weekly packages. Tennis courts are available almost everywhere, with indoor facilities in some places, Le Touquet, Cabourg and Dinard being three important centres of this sport.

For those who enjoy WALKING northern France has a great deal to offer, including marked trails for pedestrians through attractive countryside. The forests of the Boulonnais district, together with the areas round the Somme and Authie estuaries, are well prepared although, for some, there may be too much in the way of laid-out picnic areas and other niceties. There is ample scope for bird watchers. In particular, the sanctuary in the Marquenterre national park, north of the Somme estuary, visited by over 300 different species during the year, is a must for keen ornithologists.

Some Useful Addresses

Canoeing: Fédération Française de Canoe-Kayak, 87 Quai de la Marne, 94340 Joinville. Tel. 873.79.25.
Fishing: Conseil Supérieur de la Pêche, 10 Rue Peclet, 75015 Paris. Tel. 842.10.00.
Riding: Association Nationale pour le Tourisme Equestre et l'Equitation de Loisirs (ANTE), 12 Rue du Parc Royal, 75003 Paris. Tel. 277.48.56.
Golf: Fédération Française de Golf, 69 Avenue Victor-Hugo, 75116 Paris. Tel. 727.95.40 (Produces a brochure giving details of all golf courses in France).
Walking: CNSGR, 92 Rue de Clignancourt, 75018 Paris. Tel. 259.60.40.
Thalassotherapy: Syndicat National des Etablissements de Thalassothérapie, 48 Rue du Colisée, 75008 France.

In each case, the address above is that of the parent organisation. Some details of more local addresses are supplied in a leaflet entitled France for Sports and Leisure, available from the French Tourist Office, 178 Piccadilly, London W1V 0AL.

Other Pastimes

Fairs, festivities, tournaments, regattas: most resorts and cities in our region have programmes of events covering a wide range of activities, some of which attain high professional standards, from the important International Trade Fair at Lille to local sports and entertainments, from music, drama and arts festivals to traditional celebrations such as the famous *pardons* in Brittany, the *cabotan* puppets at Amiens, the parade of the giants in Douai.

For those who prefer a less highbrow recreation there is plenty of GAMBLING. Every resort with any pretentions has its casino, although it must be said that some offer a very limited choice of games. While the larger, more sophisticated establishments have roulette, chemin de fer and baccarat, there are many where you can only play *boule*, not the *pétanque*, ball-tossing variety, but a simplified form of roulette, played for lower stakes.

To the British, CHATEAUX are usually associated with the Loire but there are many historic houses further north although with generally less attention than in Britain to the associated gardens. Among the notable exceptions is the Château Bailleul near Fécamp in its lovely grounds which boasts also a fine interior; and a little further south stands the fine Château Balleroy near Argentan, an early work of François Mansart, one of the great creators of French classical architecture. Mention has been made in the author's journeys to other historic houses, including those at Miromesnil and Varengeville. Local tourist literature invariably makes a feature of interesting châteaux and gardens in the area.

There is a wide-ranging tradition of CRAFTS from the machine-made lace of Calais to that made by hand in centres such as Argentan and Bayeux; from the earthenware of Desvres to the ivory of Dieppe and the cabinet-making of Trouville. Some, like the famous Rouen *faïences* and the Arras tapestries are glories of the past, on show in museums; others, like Amien's velvet, the salt-glaze wear of Noron-la-Poterie and the pottery from Dinan and Quimper have moved more with the times, changing their product and sometimes their production methods to meet modern demands.

COOKERY courses in France are increasingly big business, the best known or, at least, most convenient to Britons being those centred on Dieppe, and that based at Hotel Univers is a good example. These short courses are often available as a package which includes the Channel crossing, accommodation and tuition.

France, always a nation of people concerned with their health, has long enjoyed fine SPAS, some known the world over for their bottled spring table waters. The traditional inland watering places, such as Bagnoles-de-l'Orne and St-Amand-les-Eaux, are being joined today by an increasing number of sea-water establishments. These include several on the northern France coast, which offer thalassotherapy treatments in pleasant surroundings for a wide range of ailments. Peripatetic readers of this book who are basically healthy but have been overdoing it at work or play may find solace and recuperation in some of the available treatments. *On doit reculer pour mieux sauter, n'est-ce pas?*

Indexes

Alphabetical Town Index

This chapter contains a two-part alphabetical index of virtually all the places in northern France mentioned in the book, with summary descriptions of the principal towns and cities visited by the author during his special journeys (chapters 1–6 inclusive).

The two parts are: A. The Ferry Ports, including a sketch map of each port at the end of the book; and B. Beyond the Ferry Ports.

In the case of the places described in Part B, distances and routes from the nearest ferry port(s) are shown; and airports are mentioned if there is a direct service from England. The hotels and restaurants named in the summaries represent the author's personal choice. Where there is none listed he has no particular recommendation. Further information about these places, beyond that in the pages of this book to which the index refers, may be sought from the local tourist offices at the given addresses.

A. The Ferry Ports

BOULOGNE, Pas de Calais — Population 50,000

From Dover (by P & O, Sealink and Hoverspeed). From *Folkestone* (by Sealink).

Office de Tourisme: Place Frédéric Sauvage, tel. (21)31.68.38 and (21)31.59.96.

A dynamic, hospitable mix of port, resort, industry and commerce, with much to interest or amuse most visitors; an unselfconscious place aware of its past but concerned more with present and future.

Features of this historic town, much damaged in World War II, include the old Haute Ville enclosed by 13th-century ramparts and gateways, with a 12th-century castle and 19th-century cathedral built partly on Roman temple and 11th-century crypt. Near the 13th-century Eglise St Nicolas is the municipal museum and art gallery. The town fronts on to river Liane with a sandy beach on the north bank: the busy dock area of France's first fishing port is entertaining. See also the Colonne de la Grande Armée nearby, topped with statue of Napoleon and offering fine views.

Inland lies pretty, undulating, partly wooded Boulonnais countryside, and 6 km to the north is the small picturesque seaside town of Wimereux.

Some Hotels. . . Faidherbe** Rue Faidherbe, tel. (21)31.60.93, 35 rooms; Metropole** Rue Thiers, tel. (21)31.54.30, 27 rooms; Alexandra** Rue Thiers, tel. (21)31.32.08, 18 rooms. . . *.and Restaurants:* Boulogne: La Matelote (Michelin rosette), La Plage, Welsh Pub. Wimereux: Atlantic (Michelin rosette, and this is also a 3-star hotel).

See pages 14–15, 21, 23–7, 29–30, 34–5, 45, 63, 118, 134–5, 145.

CALAIS, Pas de Calais — Population 80,000

From Dover (by Townsend Thoresen, Sealink and Hoverspeed). *From Folkestone* (by Sealink). *From Ramsgate* (by Hoverspeed).

Office de Tourisme: 12 Boulevard Clémenceau, tel. (21)96.62.40.

Unpromising at first, this well-worn place, and its cheerful, hospitable people soon grow on you. No northern French town has closer British ties: it was English for over 200 years and scene of the Henry VIII–François I Field of Cloth of Gold meeting; in early 19th century Nottingham lace-makers brought over their craft, many other British businesses following suit; it suffered badly during the British retreat in 1940; its pre-eminence as France's leading passenger port and stepping stone for British travellers is long established.

In its quiet way Calais has much to offer, not least its impressive Town Hall, Rodin's statue of the Burghers of Calais, a 13th-century watch tower, the church of Notre Dame, and the fine arts and war museums.

Some Hotels. . . Meurice*** 5 Rue E-Roche, tel. (21)34.57.03, 40 rooms; Richelieu** 17 Rue Richelieu, tel. (21)34.61.60, 15 rooms. . . *.and Restaurants:* La Diligence, Le Channel, Côte d'Argent. Au Monteur brasserie.

See pages 14, 16, 18, 39, 43, 45–52, 63, 118, 134, 144, 148.

CHERBOURG, Manche — Population 35,000

From Southampton or Portsmouth (by Townsend Thoresen). *From Weymouth* (by Sealink).

Airport, 13 km.

Office de Tourisme: 2 Quai Alexandre, tel. (33) 53.11.10.

A lively, noisy, congested and ever-cheerful seafaring town divided and flanked by wharves and waterways, constant reminders of Cherbourg's history and importance as a naval base and commercial port, in the former capacity often at odds with the English navy and in the latter long associated with the transatlantic passenger trade.

Much damaged as a key port in the path of the Normandy invasion of 1944, Cherbourg has been rebuilt in a rather hard, forbidding style, and the few surviving corners of the old town are more interesting than picturesque.

The fortifications, begun by Vauban, with the more recent Fort du Roule on high ground behind the town, and the extensive breakwaters, are impressive. The two museums and, when the road traffic is not too heavy, the quaysides, including those of the large yacht harbour, are worth a visit.

Some Hotels. . . Sofitel**** Gare Maritime, tel. (33)44.01.11, 80 rooms; France** 41 Avenue Maréchal Foch, tel. (33)53.10.24, 50 rooms; Torgistops** 14 Place de la République, tel. (33)43.32.32, 14 rooms; Grand* 42 Rue de la Marine, tel. (33)53.04.26, 32 rooms. . . *.and Restaurants:* Café de Paris, Vauban. Théâtre brasserie.

See pages 15, 97, 98, 99, 114–6, 120, 124, 133, 145.

DIEPPE, Seine Maritime — Population 26,000

From Newhaven (by Sealink).

Office de Tourisme: Boulevard Général de Gaulle, tel. (35)84.28.70.

Dieppe, long popular with British visitors, is a lively, hospitable, well run port and resort. The ferry ties up in the heart of the town, the central area of which lies between the harbour and a broad seafront.

With a long maritime history, Dieppe became France's first seaside resort, partly due to British patronage and partly to the fact that its beach is the nearest to Paris. While the promenade and its smart casino, overlooked by the castle containing the main museum and art gallery, are impressive, the shingle beach is in itself disappointing. The life of the town is centred on Grande Rue, a sheltered street parallel to the seafront, and the harbour quays. A war museum recalls the ill-fated Anglo-Canadian raid of 1942.

On the neighbouring Alabaster Coast lie, to the west, Fécamp, fishing port and home of Benedictine liqueur, and Etretat in its picturesque setting; and to the east Le Tréport, with its cheerful, chatty throngs. Just outside Dieppe are the interesting houses and gardens at Varengeville, and the attractive château at Miromesnil.

Some Hotels. . . Présidence**** Boulevard Verdun, tel. (35)84.31.31, 89 rooms; Univers***, furnished with antiques and has a good restaurant, 10 Boulevard Verdun, tel. (35)84.12.55, 28 rooms; Aguado*** 30 Boulevard Verdun, tel. (35)84.27.00, 53 rooms; Windsor** 18 Boulevard Verdun, tel. (35)84.15.23, 46 rooms; Select** 1 Rue Toustain, tel. (35)84.14.66, 24 rooms. . . *.and other Restaurants:* Arcades, Armorique. Petite Auberge Bistro.

See pages 14–15, 18, 85, 87–90, 94–6, 119, 122–4, 133, 148.

DUNKERQUE, Nord Population 85,000

From Dover (by Sealink). *From Ramsgate* (by Sally Viking).

Office de Tourisme. Rue Clemenceau, tel. (28) 66.79.21.

This is an important, still expanding port and city with a workaday atmosphere and not much of beauty left following World War II destruction, though its seaside suburb Malo-les-Bains has charm, character and a fine beach.

A one-time fishing port built largely on reclaimed land, Dunkerque came into prominence during the 17th century as a base for Louis XIV's warlike corsairs, including local hero Jean

Bart. There is a huge harbour and shipyard installations, boat trips being available. Best buildings include the old Town Hall, church of St Eloi, modern theatre, museum; and the Malo waterfront is attractive.

From here, the northern focus of Flanders, visit Bergues, a small market town in the heart of extensive dyke country, largely rebuilt after severe mauling in World War II.

There are good roads into Europe, including A25 via Lille.

Some Hotels. . . Europ*** 13 Rue Leughenaer, tel. (28)66.29.07, 127 rooms; Trianon** 20 Rue Colline, tel. (28)69.39.15, 13 rooms;. . .*and Restaurants:* Pingouin, at Malo. Richelieu by station, grill and fish restaurants in Europ Hotel, Victoire.

See pages 16, 36–42, 52, 119.

LE HAVRE, Seine Maritime Population 215,000

From Southampton (by P & O and Townsend Thoresen). *From Portsmouth* (by Townsend Thoresen).

Airport, 6 km.

Office de Tourisme: Place Hôtel-de-Ville, tel. (35)21.22.88.

Auguste Perret's bold scheme of reconstruction has transformed Le Havre from the Continental port most damaged of all in World War II into a spacious, modern metropolis with the new city hall on its large square as its focus, the whole in a rectangular arrangement of sometimes arcaded concrete buildings lining wide, lightly used streets and gardened squares. For anyone interested in large-scale urban planning Le Havre is well worth a visit.

Near the beach and yacht marina are the striking modern St Joseph church and the handsome new art gallery. The old cathedral is one of the few surviving buildings of distinction and there are some other older buildings towards the station and, on high ground overlooking the city and its enormous harbour, the pretty suburb of Ste Adresse and a splendid park, Montgeon forest.

Some Hotels. . . France et Bourgogne*** 21 Cours République, tel. (35)25.40.34, 31 rooms; Foch** 4 Rue Caliguy, tel. (35)42.50.69, 33 rooms;. Terminus**, with brasserie, 23 Cours République, tel. (35)25.42.48, 44 rooms. *. . .and other Restaurants:* Nice-Havrais, at Ste Adresse. Guillaume Tell and station brasseries.

See pages 14–15, 97, 99–102, 120, 124, 130–2, 145.

ROSCOFF, Finistère Population 4,000

From Plymouth (by Brittany Ferries).

Office de Tourisme: Rue Gambetta, tel. (98)69.70.70.

A cheerful, homely, close-knit agricultural town, port and seaside resort with a villagey air, wide esplanade and winding streets of warm grey stone buildings.

Connections with the sea take the form of the Paris University oceanographic research laboratory, an aquarium and much to-and-froing by fishing boats, yachts and car ferries. Roscoff is also an important vegetable export centre. The handsome 16th-century church has an interesting belfry.

Some Hotels. . . Brittany*** Rue Ste Barbe, tel. (98)69.70.78, 20 rooms; Le Triton** Roc'higou, tel. (98)61.24.44, 45 rooms; des Bains* Place Eglise, tel. (98)61.20.65, 70 rooms. The best restaurants tend to be in the hotels.

See pages 14, 16, 18, 65–7, 69, 70.

ST MALO, Ille et Vilaine Population 47,000

From Portsmouth (by Brittany Ferries).

Office de Tourisme: Port des Yachts, tel. (99)56.64.48.

A substantial, handsome walled city rising dramatically out of the sea which, without losing the character and independent spirit of a hard-working community, enjoys playing host to the tourist throngs.

From the 6th century a religious and later a maritime stronghold, St Malo was badly damaged in World War II, its extensive fortifications and principal buildings having been faithfully reconstructed. A tour of the surrounding ramparts offers delightful views of the city, its fine beaches, Dinard, the river and nearby coastlines. The castle, two forts, a cathedral and network of narrow streets are worth exploring, and the hard sandy Paramé beach is good for walking on.

Some Hotels. . . Central*** 6 Grande-Rue, tel. (99)40.87.70, 44 rooms; France-Châteaubriand** Place Châteaubriand, tel. (99)56.66.52, 50 rooms; Noguette* 9 Rue Fosse, tel. (99)40.83.57, 12 rooms. . . *.and Restaurants:* Duchesse Anne (Michelin rosette), Pomme d'Or. There are various brasseries around Place Châteaubriand. On Paramé beach: Thermes hotel and restaurant.

See pages 14–16, 18, 65–8, 82–4.

B. Beyond the Ferry Ports

ABBEVILLE, Somme Population 27,000

By Road. From Boulogne, 80 km, N1. From Dieppe, 65 km, D925 by-passing Le Tréport, then D1929.

By Rail. From Calais or Boulogne by fast trains continuing via Amiens to Paris. Branch line from Le Tréport.

Office de Tourisme: 26 Place Libération, tel. (22)24.27.92.

An old trading city on river Somme, with strong British connections. Almost wiped out in 1940 and rebuilt in a rather featureless way.

After being English for 200 years, became a French city in early 16th century. Important port and textile centre until 18th century. Local sights include 18th-century Bagatelle château and the Gothic façade of St Vulfran, also the Somme Estuary, particularly St Valéry, the Marquenterre National Park and bird sanctuary.

See pages 21, 31, 32, 120.

AGINCOURT, See Montreuil and pages 30, 118, 176.

ALABASTER COAST, See Dieppe and pages 85, 122, 154.

ALENÇON, See page 124.

AMIENS, Somme Population 135,000

By Road. From Boulogne, 125 km, N1. From Dieppe, 100 km, D1 via Neufchâtel then N29.

By Rail. From Calais or Boulogne by fast trains continuing to Paris. From Dieppe by secondary line to Serqueux changing there to Rouen-Amiens service. Served also by Paris-Amiens-Arras-Lille main line.

Office de Tourisme: Rue Jean Catelas, tel. (22)91.79.28.

A spacious, pleasant, rather staid regional capital with an outstanding riverside cathedral.

An ancient settlement on the River Somme, converted to Christianity in the 4th century, Amiens settled down as part of France in the 17th century, having been under several rulers as the bridgehead in the path of northern invaders. It was severely damaged in both World Wars.

Sights include the gothic cathedral, perhaps the largest and most beautiful in France; the high modern tower (by Perret) off the station; museums, the old circus, river walks and canal-side market gardens.

Hotel. . . Univers*** 2 Rue de Noyon, tel. (22)91.52.51, 41 rooms. . . .*and Restaurant:* La Tartine.

See pages 45, 51, 53, 60–3, 120, 134, 141, 147–8.

ANDELYS, LES, See Seine and pages 87, 95, 124, 183.

ARGENTAN, See pages 18, 98, 112, 148.

ARRAS, Pas de Calais Population 50,000

By Road. From Calais, 115 km, N43 via St Omer than A26. From Boulogne, 120 km, N1 to Montreuil then N39. Adjoins A1 Paris-Lille.

By Rail. From Calais, via Hazebrouck or via Lille. From Boulogne, by secondary line via St Pol. Served also by Paris-Amiens-Arras-Lille main line.

Office de Tourisme: Opposite rail station, tel. (21)21.53.91.

A lively city with good shopping, good eating, enough culture and several impressive relics of its past: well worth a visit for its own sake and as a base for trips to neighbouring towns and to Vimy Ridge and other World War I memorial areas.

This once-Roman town grew up around the Benedictine abbey of St-Vaast in Middle Ages, becoming a centre for wool trading, with its own soon-famous tapestry-making industry. Despite heavy bombardment in World War I, Arras still displays its spacious Flemish squares, a tribute to both 17th-century prosperity and taste and 20th-century restoration, notably the large Grande Place with 17th- and 18th-century arcaded houses on a grand scale and Place des Héros (Petite Place) with the Town Hall, founded 1460, and 250-foot belfry.

Beside the cathedral, built 1815–53, is the beautiful Abbaye St-Vaast containing the Musée de Beaux Arts, good on 17th- and 18th-century art and tapestries. See also Place Victor Hugo, polygonal but seems circular, and the old theatre.

Some Hotels. . . Univers*** 3 Place Croix Rouge, tel. (21)21.34.01, historic building with courtyard, 33 rooms; Moderne*** 1 Boulevard Faidherbe, tel. (21)23.39.57, 45 rooms. . . *.and Restaurants:* L'Ambassadeur (Michelin rosette) in station building. Grandes Arcades brasserie.

See pages 39, 43, 45, 51, 53, 56–8, 120, 135, 137, 141, 148.

ARROMANCHES, See Bayeux and page 111.

AUDIERNE, See Quimper and pages 66, 71–2, 178.

AULNE, RIVER, See Châteaulin and pages 71, 145.

AUTHIE, RIVER, See pages 30, 145, 146.

AVRANCHES, See Granville and pages 98, 113–4, 172.

BAGNOLES DE L'ORNE, See pages 112, 149.

BAILLEUL, CHATEAU, See page 148.

BALLEROY, CHÂTEAU, See page 187.

BAYEUX, Calvados Population 15,000

By Road. From Cherbourg, 90 km, N13. From Havre, 140 km, N182 across Tancarville bridge, then A13 to Caen, thence N13. From St Malo, 180 km, D4 via Dol, then N175 to Villedieu after which D999 via St Lô, then D572.

By Rail. From Cherbourg by Paris-bound fast trains. From Le Havre by Paris-bound fast trains changing at Rouen and again at Caen. From St Malo changing at Dol on to the Caen-bound service from Rennes.

By Bus. From Le Havre, direct service by Courriers Normands to Caen, thence by train.

Office de Tourisme: 1 Rue des Cuisiniers, tel. (31)92.16.26.

An old-established, former Roman community, a bishopric since the 4th-century, the place where Harold's miscalculation led to William the Conqueror's invasion of England and the first town to be liberated by the advancing Allied armies in 1944, Bayeux has a long and interesting history.

Its famous tapestry, depicting the Norman conquest of England, is one of northern France's best known tourist attractions. With its very fine Norman Gothic cathedral, some splendid old mansions and several quaint old streets, this is a great place for wandering in.

The dividing line between the British-Canadian and the American sectors of the D-Day beaches lies just to the north of Bayeux, and nearby is Arromanches with the most substantial of the invasion museums and a vantage point for the Mulberry harbours.

See pages 18, 97–8, 110–11, 129, 148.

BENODET, See Quimper and pages 66–7, 71–2.

BERCK, See Le Touquet and pages 21, 29, 145.

BERGUES, See Dunkerque and page 41.

BETHUNE, See pages 39, 52, 62.

BOULONNAIS, THE, See Boulogne and pages 29–30, 146, 151.

BREST, Finistère Population 172,000

By Road. From Roscoff, 70 km, D788. From St Malo, 235 km, N137, N176 via Lamballe then N12.

By Rail. From Roscoff via Morlaix, from St Malo via Rennes, thence by Paris-Brest main line. Alternatively from St Malo, by branch lines via Dol to Lamballe, thence by Paris-Brest main line.

Airport, 10 km.

Office de Tourisme: Place Liberté, tel. (98)44.24.96.

This is a seafaring and industrial city, with all the amenities to be expected of a major provincial centre, but interesting more for its history than for what it can show today. The views from Brest across its roadstead towards the rugged Finistère coastlines are an important feature.

Brest has always had strategic importance and, from the 17th century, has been France's leading naval port. Its commercial port is today growing in importance alongside the naval base. Largely destroyed while in German hands in World War II, the rebuilt town is a pleasant if unexciting arrangement of wide streets, squares and parks. Sights include the old castle and various museums.

Across the roadstead is the Crozon peninsula, a picturesque rocky promontory with a pretty hinterland and some attractive south facing beaches. There is a ferry service from Brest.

Some Hotels. . . Voyageurs*** 15 Avenue Clémenceau, tel. (98)80.25.73, 39 rooms; Vauban** 17 Avenue Clémenceau, tel. (98)46.06.88, 53 rooms. . . *.and Restaurants:* Hôtel Voyageurs restaurant (Michelin rosette) and brasserie, rail station restaurant.

See pages 65–7, 71, 73–5, 133.

BRIQUEBEC, See page 114.

CABOURG, See Deauville and pages 97, 107–8, 146.

CAEN, Calvados — Population 125,000

By Road. From Le Havre, 110 km, N182 across Tancarville bridge, then A13. From Cherbourg, 120 km, N13.

By Rail. From Le Havre by Paris-bound fast trains changing at Rouen for trains direct to Caen. From Cherbourg by Paris-bound fast trains.

By Bus. From Le Havre, direct service along the coast by Courriers Normands.

Airport, 6 km.

Office de Tourisme: Place St Pierre, tel. (31)86.27.65

Severely damaged in World War II, Caen has been reconstructed skilfully in traditional style, the new blending well with what remains of the old, the general impression being of a spacious, good-looking modern city aware of but not overawed by its history.

The chief reminders of the past are the splendid castle and Abbayes aux Hommes and aux Dames, in their commanding positions. The town was a stronghold of William the Conqueror, but it fell to his wife, Matilda, to rule in Caen whenever her husband was busy running his new domain across the Channel, and the two abbeys, one for men and the other for women, remain as magnificent reminders of their good works.

There survive also, among other religious buildings, the fine old church of St Pierre, a few squares and streets with ancient houses; while the more recently made boulevards, gardens and precincts, with their background of intruding docks and basins, enhance the dignity of this distinguished and progressive city.

Some Hotels. . . Moderne*** 116 Boulevard Maréchal Leclerc, tel. (31)86.04.23, 57 rooms; France** 10 Rue Gare, tel. (31)82.16.99, 41 rooms; Royal** 1 Place République, tel. (31)86.55.33, 45 rooms. *. . .and Restaurants:* Relais des Gourmets (Michelin rosette), part of a 5-star hotel, 15 Rue Géole, tel. (31)86.06.01; L'Assiette, near castle; Buffet de la Gare. La Coupole brasserie, facing St Pierre, bar and brasserie in Royal hotel.

See pages 18, 97–8, 102, 108–11, 120, 124, 126–9, 142, 145.

CANCALE, See page 121.

CANCHE, RIVER, See Montreuil and pages 28, 32, 145.

CAUDEBEC, See Seine and pages 85, 90–1, 183.

CHATEAULIN, Finistère Population 6,000

By Road. From Roscoff, 60 km, D788 via Lesneven then D770, N165. From St Malo, 220 km, N137, N176 via Lamballe then N12 via Guingamp, after which D787 becoming N164 at Carhaix-Plouguer.

By Rail. From Roscoff via Morlaix, from St Malo via Rennes, thence main line from Paris changing at Brest on to secondary line trains which continue to Quimper.

Office de Tourisme: La Mairie, tel. (98)86.02.11

This is an inviting small riverside town with handsome tree-lined boulevard and a happy arrangement of shops, houses and public buildings.

Its attractive river, the Aulne, famous for its salmon fishing and much of it navigable, passes through pretty countryside to emerge into the Brest roadstead. Douarnenez, a gateway to the Raz promontory, is on the nearby coast.

The two-star Au Bon Accueil hotel and restaurant is by the river 2 km downstream, tel. (98)86.15.77, 59 rooms.

See pages 65–7, 71–2.

CONCARNEAU, See page 121.

CORNICHE NORMANDE, See Deauville and pages 97, 103.

COTE FLEURIE, See Deauville and pages 107, 108.

COUTAINVILLE, See Granville and pages 98, 114.

COUTANCES, See Granville and pages 98, 114, 124, 129.

CRECY, See Montreuil and pages 25, 118.

CREUILLY, See page 129.

CREVECOEUR-EN-AUGE, See page 130.

CROZON PENINSULA, See Brest and pages 65, 67, 70–1, 73.

D-DAY BEACHES, See Bayeux and page 111.

DEAUVILLE, Calvados Population 6,000

By Road. From Le Havre, 75 km, N182, across Tancarville bridge, after which N178, N175 via Pont-l'Evêque then N177.

By Rail. From Le Havre, by Paris-bound fast train changing at

Rouen on to Caen line; changing again at Lisieux on to branch line.

By Bus. From Le Havre, direct service along coast by Courriers Normands, this way being faster than the series of trains.

Airport, 3 km.

Office de Tourisme: Résidence Desmoulins, tel. (31)88.21.43.

Deauville, leading resort of the Côte Fleurie, has long been one of France's most elegant watering places, its luxurious sea-front hotels, fashionable casinos and racecourse, and many large neo-Norman-Gothic villas bearing witness to grander days. However, Deauville still flourishes as a retreat for the wealthy, the high social peak in August being centred on the famous Grand Prix race meeting, although nowadays, in the summer, particularly at weekends, the resort fills up with cheerful crowds of all and sundry who parade along the famous beachside Planches, around the vast new yacht harbour and throng the many bars, cafés and restaurants.

Adjoining Deauville, across the Touques, is the older, brasher resort of Trouville, in its picturesque setting; and a few kilometres further east along the Corniche Normande is the ancient port of Honfleur, with its well known enclosed harbour, long favoured by British yachtsmen. The leading resort west-ward is Cabourg, a quiet, once-elegant and quite charming small seaside town with an unusual street pattern which, on the map, resembles a lady's open fan.

Some Hotels. . . Deauville: Normandy***** Rue Jean Mermoz, tel. (31)88.09.21, 326 rooms; Royal***** Boulevard Cornuché, tel. (31)88.16.41, 320 rooms; PLM*** Boulevard Cornuché, tel. (31)88.62.62, 64 rooms; La Fresnaye*** 81 Avenue République, tel. (31)88.09.71, 14 rooms; Continental** 1 Rue Désiré-le-Hoc, tel. (31)88.21.06, 49 rooms; Nid d'Eté** 121 Avenue République, tel. (31)88.36.67, 24 rooms. Apartments at Résidence

Orion. Trouville: Bellevue*** 1 Place Maréchal Foch, tel. (31)88.14.85, 67 rooms. Cabourg: Grand**** Promenade Marcel Proust, tel. (31)91.01.79, 70 rooms; Paris** 39 Avenue Mer, tel. (31)91.31.34, 23 rooms. . . *.and Restaurants:* Deauville: Ciro's (lunch only), Saratoga, Désirée-Deauville, Chez Camillo, and in most hotels. Chantilly and Drakkar brasseries.

See pages 18, 97, 103–7, 122, 130, 146.

DINAN, See Dinard and pages 18, 66, 68, 78–9, 144, 148.

DINARD, Ille et Vilaine Population 10,000

By Road. From St Malo, 7 km, D168. From Roscoff, 190 km, D58 via Morlaix then N12 to Lamballe, after which N176 via Dinan, continuing on D766. From Cherbourg, 200 km, N13 via Carentan then N174 via St Lô, continuing on D999 via Villedieu then N175, N176 to Dol, thence D4.

By Rail. From St Malo, no suitable service but there is a direct bus from St Malo Station. You may reach St Malo: from Roscoff, via Morlaix and Rennes or via Lamballe and Dol, with changes of train at each of these places; from Cherbourg, by bus to Coutances connecting there with the Caen-Rennes service, changing off that at Dol for the branch line to St Malo.

By Ferry. From St Malo across the River Rance.

Airport, 6 km.

Office de Tourisme: Boulevard Féart, tel. (99)46.94.12.

Originally a fishing village, Dinard developed from mid-19th century into a well-bred resort, 'gem' of the Emerald Coast. On a lush promontory between estuary and open sea, it offers endearing reminders of a fashionable tennis-club hey-day and a warm welcome to visitors from its laconically good humoured people.

Separated only by the Rance estuary Dinard and St Malo, with their distinctive characters, together make an ideal holiday destination. Tennis continues to be a leading Dinard sport and it is a good centre for coastal walking.

Nearby, inviting seaside resorts include St Cast, Sables d'Or and Le Val André. Some 20 km inland is Dinan, a beautifully preserved walled city in a fine setting above the River Rance: this may be reached by direct boat or bus, or from St Malo by train, changing at the pleasant market town of Dol.

Some Hotels. . . Reine Hortense****, rather exceptional, 19 Rue Malouine, tel. (99)46.54.31, 10 rooms; Grand**** 46 Avenue George V, tel. (99)46.10.28, 100 rooms; Crystal***, with adjoining apartments, 15 Rue Malouine, tel. (99)46.66.71, 19 rooms; Printania** 5 Avenue George V, tel. (99)46.13.07, 77 rooms; Bains** 38 Avenue George V, tel. (99)46.13.71, 40 rooms. . . *.and Restaurants:* the hotels Grand and Printania have satisfactory restaurants and there is cheaper eating in downtown brasseries. There is more choice in St Malo.

See pages 18, 66—8, 79–82, 146.

DIVES, See pages 18, 108, 117.

DOL, See Dinard and pages 68, 79.

DOUAI, Nord — Population 50,000

By Road. From Dunkerque, 105 km: from ferry port, N1, N355 then N225 joining A25; from town, D916 also joining A25: on to

Lille there joining A1 to Noyelles, after which N43. From Calais 130 km, N43 joining A26 near Lillers then C26 around Lens into W43. From Boulogne, 145 km, N1 to Montreuil then N39, joining N50 at Arras.

By Rail. From Dunkerque and Calais, fast trains, change at Lille. From Boulogne, secondary line via St Pol and Arras. Served also by Paris-Amiens-Lille main line.

Office de Tourisme: 70 Place d'Armes, tel. (27)87.26.63.

This ancient town is a chatty and rather congested industrial 'capital', with some attractive remnants of its past history. Under several rulers until union with France in 1667, it was for a while the seat of the Flanders parliament. The Roman Catholic bible was first translated into English here but Douai's intellectual life diminished when its cosmopolitan university was transferred to Lille in 1887.

See the palais de justice, former seat of the Flanders parliament, the ancient charterhouse, now housing the town museum, the famous belfry and large church. Although the town was much damaged in both World Wars, impressive canal-side buildings remain.

Some Restaurants: La Terrasse, Etna Pizzeria, station buffet.

See pages 43, 45, 51, 58–9, 135, 137, 147.

DOUARNENEZ, See Châteaulin and pages 66, 72, 121.

DUCLAIR, See Seine and pages 92, 183.

EMERALD COAST, See Dinard and pages 79–80.

ETAPLES, See Le Touquet and pages 23, 27, 30, 34.

ETRETAT, See Dieppe and pages 85, 90, 122, 123.

FÉCAMP, See Dieppe and pages 85, 90, 148.

GIVERNY, See page 123.

GOUET, RIVER, See page 145.

GRANVILLE, Manche Population 15,000

By Road. From St Malo, 90 km, D4 via Dol then N175 to Avranches, after which D973. From Cherbourg, 105 km, N13 via Valognes then D2 to Coutances, after which D971.

By Rail. From St Malo changing first at Dol on to the Rennes-Caen and second at Folligny on to the Paris-Granville service. From Cherbourg, by bus to Coutances connecting there with the Caen-Rennes rail service changing off that at Folligny on to the Paris-Granville service.

Office de Tourisme: 15 Rue Georges Clemenceau, tel. (33)50.02.67.

A quite spectacular port, resort and one-time fort, built on a huge slab of rock jutting into the Atlantic, calling itself with becoming modesty and a blind eye to its somewhat non-Mediterranean climate, the 'Monaco of the North', Granville is an enjoyable mix of quaint old town, ramparts, gardens, harbour and beaches.

Visits may be made by sea to Jersey and the Iles de Chausey.

From Avranches, 25 km south, towards St Malo, a very agreeable small town with a cathedral, castle and attractive gardens, excursions may be made by road and, sometimes, by air the 22 km on to the famous, exceptionally picturesque Mont St Michel abbey on its great sea-girt rock.

At Coutances, 30 km north, towards Cherbourg, in a hill-top setting, is an outstanding Norman Gothic cathedral; and near that town is the pleasant seaside resort of Coutainville.

Some Hotels. . . Granville: Des Bains** 19 Rue Clemenceau, tel. (33)50.17.31, 60 rooms; Michelet** 5 Rue Michelet, tel. (33)50.06.55, 18 rooms. Avranches: Croix d'Or** 83 Rue Constitution, tel. (33)58.04.88, 30 rooms; Auberge St Michel, 7 Place Général Patton, tel. (33)58.01.91, 24 rooms. Coutances: Grand** Place de la Gare, tel. (33)45.06.55, 25 rooms. . . *.and Restaurants:* Granville: Normandy-Chaumière brasserie. Avranches and Coutances: in the hotels.

See pages 18, 98, 112–3.

GRAVELINES, See pages 41, 52.

HARDELOT, See Le Touquet and pages 21, 29.

HESDIN, See Montreuil and pages 21, 30, 32.

HONFLEUR, See Deauville and pages 97, 102–3, 122–4, 130–1, 167.

HOULGATE, See page 107.

JUMIEGES, See Seine and pages 85, 92, 129.

LANNION, Côtes du Nord Population 20,000

By Road. From Roscoff, 70 km, D58 via Morlaix then D786. From St Malo, 140 km, N137, N176 via Lamballe then N12 via Guingamp, after which D767.

By Rail. From Roscoff to Morlaix, thence Brest-Rennes-Paris main line changing at Plouaret on to branch line. From St Malo to Rennes, or via Dol to Lamballe, thence Paris-Rennes-Brest main line changing at Plouaret on to branch line.

Office de Tourisme: Quai d'Aiguillon, tel. (96)37.07.35.

A neat, welcoming, compact riverside town with tidy pedestrianised shopping alleys and a choice selection of old buildings.

From here tour the attractive western end of the Cornish-style Pink Granite Coast, including the resorts of Perros-Guirec, Trégastel and Trébeurden.

See pages 18, 65, 67, 75–6.

LESSAY, See page 114.

LILLE, Nord Population 200,000

By Road. From Dunkerque, 70 km; from ferry port N1, N355, then N225 joining A25; from town, D916 also joining A25. From Calais, 110 km, N43 via St Omer, then N42 joining A25 near Bailleul. From Boulogne, 120 km, N42 joining A25 at Bailleul. Adjoins A1 Paris-Lille-Antwerp and (continuation of A25) A27 Lille-Brussels.

By Rail. From Dunkerque or Calais, direct main-line trains, some continuing to Strasbourg, Basel. From Boulogue by secondary line via St Pol. Terminus of Paris-Amiens-Arras-Lille main line.

Airport, 10 km.

Office de Tourisme: Palais Rihour, tel. (20)30.81.00.

An industrial and commercial city of great importance with some impressive features, not least its Musée des Beaux Arts, but a little sad and unkempt in feeling: a convenient base but otherwise somewhere for the businessman more than the tourist.

Founded on an island, and thus originally 'l'isle', Lille became in the middle ages a prosperous Flemish textile city. After passing through various hands, it was captured for France by Louis XIV in 1667, to be fortified extensively by Vauban in 1708. The 19th century was a heyday, when it grew and prospered as a hub of the French industrial revolution. General Charles de Gaulle was born here in 1890.

Impressive buildings in central area include theatre, stock exchange, cathedral and the museum; in the old town, the Hospice Comtesse and Palais de Justice; and just off centre, the citadelle. The railway station is said to be the most extensive in France, Lille's large international exhibition centre being close by.

Some Hotels. . . Grand Hôtel Bellevue*** 5 Rue Jean-Roisin, tel. (20)57.45.86, 80 rooms; Mapotel Carlton*** 3 Rue de Paris, tel. (20)55.24.11, 70 rooms. *. . .and Restaurants:* Le Compostelle. Vega Store brasserie. Rail station buffet.

See pages 39, 43, 45, 51–6, 58, 136–8, 141, 147.

LISIEUX, Calvados — Population 27,000

By Road. From Le Havre, 80 km, N182, across Tancarville

bridge, N178, N175 via Pont-L'Evêque, then D579.

By Rail. From Le Havre by Paris-bound fast trains changing at Rouen for trains which continue to Caen.

Office de Tourisme: 11 Rue Alençon, tel. (31)62.08.41.

Apart from its splendid French Gothic cathedral and a few streets of old timbered houses, Lisieux was completely destroyed by air attacks during the Allied advances in 1944. Best known as a religious centre, and particularly for its stoic young Ste Thérèse, Lisieux attracts numerous pilgrims, the headquarters of this activity being an imposing modern basilica, on the terrace of which Pope Jean-Paul II has celebrated mass.

But Lisieux today is primarily the important if small-scale 'capital' of a busy industrial and agricultural district and, being in that guise a fairly ordinary 20th-century town, its appeal to the general run of tourist is probably somewhat limited.

See pages 97, 106–7, 120, 154.

LOUVIERS, See page 129.

MALO-LES-BAINS, See Dunkerque and pages 40–1.

MARAIS AUDOMAROIS, See St Omer and page 53.

MARQUENTERRE, THE, See Abbeville and pages 31, 146.

MIROMESNIL CHATEAU, See Dieppe and pages 85, 89, 148.

MONTREUIL, Pas de Calais   Population 3,000

By Road. From Boulogne, 40 km, N1.

By Rail. From Boulogne by secondary line which continues via St Pol to Arras.

Office de Tourisme: La Mairie, tel. (21)06.01.33.

A small, picturesque, walled market town, dating from an 8th-century monastery, with castle, all in pretty setting and full of present-day bustle: a fortress town since 10th century and, until river Canche silted up, a leading seaport.

The Citadelle, originally 16th-century, and adjoining ramparts have wide rural views; there are some old streets and houses and a statue of Haig, Commander of the British Forces, who was stationed here in World War I.

Montreuil is also a convenient base for the small town of Hesdin, with its several ancient buildings; the old battlefields of Crécy and Agincourt; and an attractive river and forest countryside.

Some Hotels. . . Château de Montreuil****, with recommended restaurant, Chaussée Capucins, tel. (21)06.00.11, 14 rooms; Central** 7 Rue du Change, tel. (21)06.10.33, 10 rooms. *. . .and Restaurants:* Brasserie Darnetal.

See pages 21, 23, 31, 32, 34.

MONT-ST-MICHEL, See Granville and pages 98, 113.

MORGAT, See pages 65, 70.

MORLAIX, Finistère   Population 20,000

By Road. From Roscoff, 30 km, D58. From St Malo, 160 km,

N137, N176 via Lamballe, then N12.

By Rail. From Roscoff, direct branch line. From St Malo via Rennes, thence main line from Paris which continues to Brest.

Airport, 5 km.

Office de Tourisme: Place des Otages, tel. (98)62.14.94.

A snug, picturesque and historic small trading town and port in a deep river valley with attractive buildings and a pleasantly busy ambience, the whole bestrode by a tremendous railway viaduct.

Hotel. . . Europe** in town centre, with cheerful brasserie, 1 Rue Aiguillon, tel. (98)62.11.99, 64 rooms. . . *.and Restaurant:* Le Coquin.

See pages 18, 65–7, 75, 142.

ODET, RIVER, See Quimper and page 72.

OPAL COAST, See Le Touquet and page 29.

PARAME BEACH, See St Malo and pages 66, 84.

PENHIR POINT, See page 65.

PERROS-GUIREC, See Lannion and pages 65, 67, 76.

PINK GRANITE COAST, See Lannion and pages 65, 75–6, 80.

PONT-AVEN, See pages 121, 133.

PONT L'EVEQUE, See page 106.

QUIMPER, Finistère Population 60,000

By Road. From Roscoff, 90 km, D788 via Lesneven then D770, N165. From St Malo, 230 km, N137, N176 via Lamballe, then N12 to Guingamp after which D787, becoming N164 at Carhaix-Plouguer. After 20 km turn off down D72 to Briec thence D785.

By Rail. From Roscoff via Morlaix or from St Malo via Rennes, thence by the main line from Paris, changing at Brest on to Quimper secondary line.

Airport, 7 km.

Office de Tourisme: 3 Rue Roi-Gradlon, tel. (98)95.04.69.

An important city on the River Odet with an inviting mix of sights and amenities, and a convenient centre for the western end of southern Brittany. Besides its fine Gothic cathedral, the most complete of its kind in Brittany, there are hillside gardens, markets, a museum and art gallery.

Nearby is the spectacular Raz promontory and the pleasant seaside town of Audierne with its extensive nearby beaches.

A few kilometres downstream, at the mouth of the picturesque River Odet, is Benodet, a delightful small estuary town, and a good base for this attractive south-facing coastline and its hinterland, all well suited to young families and visitors in search of the alfresco life.

Hotels, restaurants and self-catering facilities in this area are numerous.

See pages 66–7, 71–2, 133, 148.

RANCE, RIVER, See Dinard and pages 78, 82.

RAZ PROMONTORY, See Châteaulin, Quimper and pages 66, 71–2.

RENNES, Ille et Vilaine Population 205,000

By Road. From St Malo, 70 km, N137. From Roscoff, 210 km, D58 via Morlaix then N12. From Cherbourg, 210 km, N13 via Carentan then N174 via St Lô, continuing on D999 via Villedieu, then N175.

By Rail. From St Malo, by direct branch line. From Roscoff via Morlaix then Brest-Rennes-Paris main line. From Cherbourg, by bus to Coutances connecting there with the Caen-Rennes rail service.

Airport, 7 km.

Office de Tourisme: Pont de Nemours, tel. (99)79.01.98.

A very large city, more or less in two halves, including a small but attractive medieval quarter; an important cultural, scientific and manufacturing centre; and France's gateway into Brittany.

In 1491, Charles VIII besieged Rennes for the hand of Anne, Duchess of Brittany, her territories joining France as a result of their union. Much of the city was destroyed by fire in 1720, to be rebuilt largely on a rectangular pattern.

The cathedral stands in the medieval quarter, on the edge of which is the fine palais de justice. Nearby is the handsome Town Hall and, on the other side of the river, the principal museums. The Thabor Garden offers a pleasant retreat. For tourists the liveliest area adjoins the rail station and administrative quarter of the city.

The well-preserved old-world town of Vitré with its striking castle lies 40 km east of Rennes on the main railway and close to the main road to Paris.

Some Hotels. . . Du Guesclin*** 5 Place Gare, tel. (99)79.47.47, 66 rooms; Cheval d'Or** Place Gare, tel. (99)30.25.80, 40 rooms; Voyageurs** 28 Avenue Janvier, tel. (99)30.34.36, 32 rooms. . . *.and Restaurants:* Corsaire in old quarter, rail station restaurant.

See pages 65, 66, 68, 76–7, 133, 137, 142.

ROUEN, Seine Maritime Population 120,000

By Road. From Dieppe, 60 km, N27. From Le Havre, 90 km, N15.

By Rail. From Dieppe or Le Havre by direct fast trains.

Office de Tourisme: 25 Place Cathédrale, tel. (35)71.41.77.

A majestic and historic city, ringed by hills, its ancient centre separated by the wide Seine from the more modern administrative quarter, the former itself divided by a main street named Rue Jeanne d'Arc in commemoration of Rouen's great heroine. Much of the old part of the city comprises a dazzling example of imaginative and extensive restoration, the original medieval heart with its many half-timbered houses being once again almost intact.

Rouen, originally a Roman city, historically site of the first bridge going up the Seine, is a leading manufacturing, administrative and cultural centre with an important port, its style and substance being more that of a capital than of a regional city; and, accordingly, it has a range of amenities and attractions to interest every visitor.

Besides perambulation around the restored and pedestrianised alleyways and squares, there are the cathedral, a breathtaking example of French Gothic architecture begun in the 12th century, and among other churches the splendid St Ouen, St Maclou (still being restored) and St Godard (with its wonderful stained glass). Other sights include the Gros Horloge, Palais de Justice and City Hall, to say nothing of a wealth of museums and an exceptional art gallery.

Vantage points with sweeping views of city, river and countryside include that on Ste Catherine hill, just to the south east.

Some Hotels. . . By rail station, Dieppe*** Place Bernard Tissot, tel. (35)71.96.00, 44 rooms; Astrid** 121 Rue Jeanne d'Arc, tel. (35)71.75.88, 40 rooms. In old quarter, Frantel***** Rue Croix de Fer, tel. (35)98.06.98, 125 rooms; Cathédrale** 12 Rue St Romain, tel. (35)71.57.95, 25 rooms. *. . .and Restaurants:* Château d'O, Quatre Saisons (in hotel Dieppe), Havre. Pascaline brasserie.

See pages 85, 87, 92–4, 118, 122, 123–6, 129, 130, 132, 134, 137, 142, 148.

SABLES D'OR, See Dinard and page 80.

ST AMAND LES EAUX, See page 149.

ST CAST, See Dinard and page 80.

ST LO, See page 119.

ST MARTIN DE BOSCHERVILLE, See page 129.

ST OMER, Pas de Calais Population 18,000

By Road. From Calais, 40 km, N43. From Dunkerque, 40 km, D916 via Bergues then D982. From Boulogne, 55 km, N42. A26 starts nearby.

By Rail. From Calais on main line to Lille.

Office de Tourisme: Hotel de Ville, Place Foch, tel. (21)98.40.88.

A distinguished small canal-side town, sometimes called the 'Venice of the North', stopping-off point for the peaceful network of small lakes and waterways which include Le Marais Audomarois.

The town grew up around the 7th-century St Bertin abbey; by the middle ages, it was an important cathedral city; and it became French in 17th century. Trade increased with the growth of canals, of which it is a hub. St Omer was badly damaged in World War II but soon regained its poise.

Sights include the cathedral, begun in the 13th century, St Bertin ruins, the museum and some picturesque gardens. Boat trips may be made on the waterways.

Some Hotels. . . Bretagne** 2 Place du Vainquai, tel. (21)38.25.78. . . *.and Restaurants:* Le Cygne, Le Truye qui File, Chez Henriette.

See pages 43, 52–3, 145.

ST SAUVEUR LE VICOMTE, See page 114.

ST THEGONNEC, See page 75.

ST VALERY, See Abbeville and pages 21, 31, 32, 117.

STE MERE EGLISE, See page 111.

SARRE, RIVER, See page 145.

SEINE, RIVER, This note refers to one stretch down river from Rouen, including Caudebec, 35 km, and Villequier, and to Les Andelys which lies 48 km up river.

CAUDEBEC Population 3,000

By Road. From Le Havre, 55 km, N182, D982.

By Rail. Nearest station Yvetot, 14 km, on Havre-Rouen-Paris main line.

Office de Tourisme: Rue de la Boucherie, tel. (35)96.11.12.

Small town on beautiful bend of Seine valley facing Brotonne forest, with a fine old church; othewise largely rebuilt since war damage. Attractive riverside promenade with hotels, including Marine*** and Normandie**, both with restaurants.

VILLEQUIER, four km away on a neighbouring reach of the river, is a charming village, backed by high ground offering lovely views, with the lavish, château-style hotel Domaine de Villequier****, with restaurant. The very pleasant riverside amenities include the small, pubby Hôtel de France*.

The ancient abbey of Jumièges and pleasant village of Duclair lie between Caudebec and Rouen on the D982 road.

LES ANDELYS Population 8,000

By Road. From Rouen, N14 then D1. No convenient access by rail.

Office de Tourisme: Rue Philippe-Auguste, tel. (32)54.10.52.

A well known river resort in two halves with an interesting

history and some good buildings including the Chaîne d'Or**, a rambling, country-style hotel and restaurant by the water.

See pages 85, 86, 90–2, 103, 122, 125.

SOMME, RIVER, See Abbeville, Amiens and pages 31, 145, 146.

SUISSE NORMANDE, See page 112.

TANCARVILLE BRIDGE, See Deauville and pages 90, 102.

TREBEURDEN, See Lannion and pages 65, 76, 145.

TREGASTEL See Lannion and page 76.

TOUQUES, RIVER, See Deauville and pages 106, 107.

LE TOUQUET, Pas de Calais Population 6,000

By Road. From Boulogne, 30 km, D940.

By Rail. Nearest station Etaples, 5 km. From Calais or Boulogne by fast Paris-bound trains. There is a secondary line via St Pol to Arras.

Airport, 3 km.

Office de Tourisme: Palais de l'Europe, tel. (21)05.21.65.

A bracing, confident seaside resort, the most sophisticated in north-east France, once haunt of fashionable Britons, now offering amenities to suit all tastes.

Little more than a century old, Le Touquet developed from a small settlement of villas, built in the shelter of a specially planted forest, alongside an exceptionally wide, firm sandy beach.

On offer are numerous sporting facilities, notably golf, tennis (including covered courts), sand-yachting, horse-racing; also spa facilities and a smart casino.

It is known as the 'jewel' of the Opal Coast; its nearby smaller resorts including Berck and Hardelot.

Some Hotels. . . Westminster**** opposite Casino, tel. (21)05.19.66, 145 rooms; Côte d'Opale*** on sea front, tel. (21)05.08.11, 28 rooms; Plage** on sea front, tel. (21)05.03.22, 25 rooms; Novotel-Thalamer**** south end of beach, tel. (21)05.24.00, 104 rooms; Manoir*** by golf courses, tel. (21)05.20.22, 47 rooms. . . *.and Restaurants:* Flavio (Michelin rosette), l'Orée, l'Escale at airport.

See pages 21, 23, 27–8, 33, 34, 145, 146.

LE TREPORT, See Dieppe and pages 87, 95.

TROUVILLE, See Deauville and pages 97, 105, 106, 122, 124, 148.

VAL ANDRE, See Dinard and page 80.

VALENCIENNES, Nord Population 45,000

By Road. From Dunkerque, 120 km; from ferry port, N1, N355, then N225 joining A25; from town, D916 also joining A25. After Lille join C27 then N49. From Calais, 155 km, N43 via St Omer, then N42 joining A25 near Bailleul. After Lille join C27 then N49. From Boulogne, 170 km, N1 to Montreuil then N39 joining N50 at Arras, and from Douai N45.

By Rail. From Dunkerque or Calais, direct main line trains through Lille. From Boulogne, secondary line via St Pol and Arras.

Office de Tourisme: 1 Rue Askièvre, tel. (27)46.22.99.

A busy, self-assured city, sometimes known as the 'Athens of the North' and now, officially, as *'Une Ville pour ses Habitants'*, Valenciennes has an interesting range of amenities in a cosmopolitan ambience.

A city of the middle ages, lace-making centre, home of artists and sculptors, and now a busy manufacturing community, there are fine boulevards, a convivial main square facing the Town Hall's Flemish Rennaissance-style façade and an interesting museum.

Some Hotels. . . Mapotel Grand*** Place de la Gare, tel. (20)46.32.01, 90 rooms; Bristol** 2 Avenue Lattre de Tassigny, tel. (20)46.24.09. . . *.and Restaurants:* Buffet-Gare (Michelin rosette), La Dodenne, La Coupole brasserie, La Paix café.

See pages 43, 45, 52, 53, 58, 60, 135–7.

VARENGEVILLE, See Dieppe and pages 85, 90, 123, 148.

VILLEQUIER, See Seine and pages 85, 91.

VIMY RIDGE, See Arras and pages 58, 120.

GENERAL INDEX

French Channel Port Maps

KEY

for the following Maps

Principal routes through town centre

Roads

Rivers/Canals

Railway station

G - Police station

P - Car Parks

H - Hospitals

Tourist Information

M Museums

The following maps are to give an indication rather than exact location of places

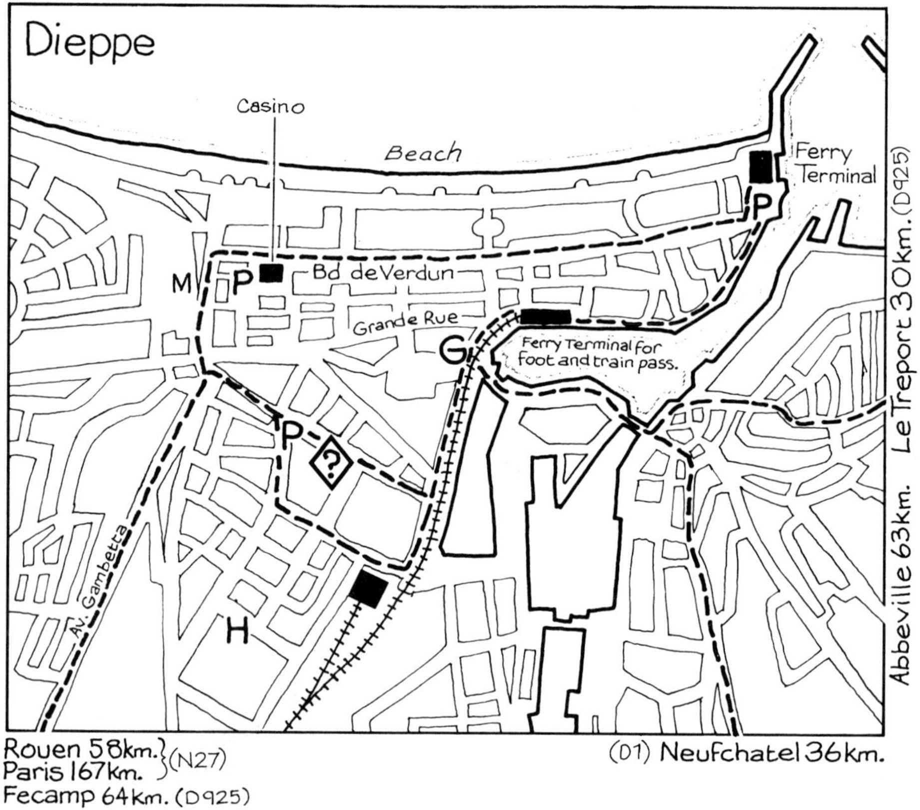
Dieppe
Casino
Beach
Ferry Terminal
P
M
Bd de Verdun
Grande Rue
G
Ferry Terminal for foot and train pass.
?
Av. Gambetta
H
Rouen 58km.
Paris 167km.
(N27)
Fecamp 64km. (D925)
(D1) Neufchatel 36km.
Abbeville 63km.
Le Treport 30km. (D925)

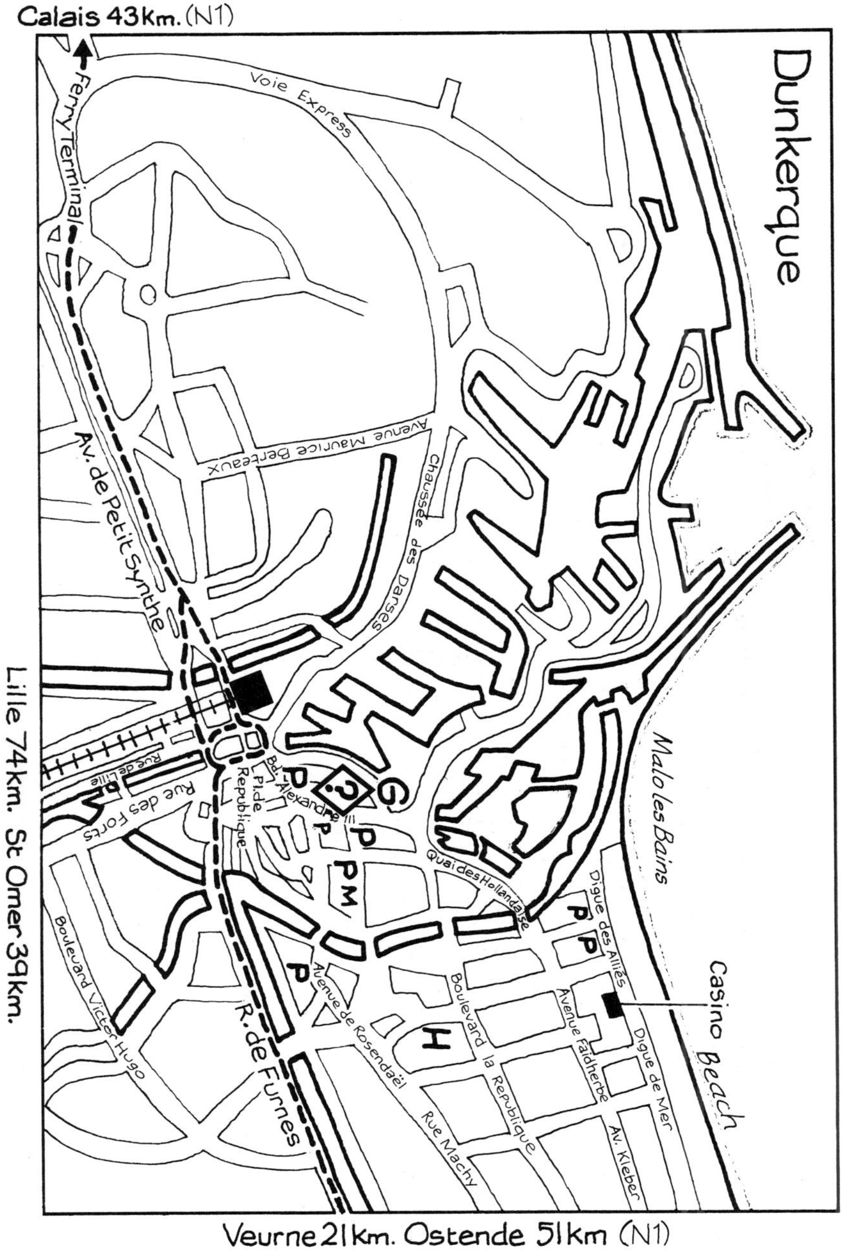
Calais 43km. (N1)
Dunkerque
Voie Express
Ferry Terminal
Avenue Maurice Berteaux
Chaussée des Darses
Av. de Petit Synthe
Rue de Lille
Rue des Forts
Pl. de Republique
Bd. Alexandre III
Quai des Hollandaise
Malo les Bains
Digue des Alliés
Casino
Beach
Avenue Faidherbe
Digue de Mer
Boulevard la Republique
Avenue de Rosendaël
Boulevard Victor Hugo
R. de Furnes
Rue Machy
Av. Kleber
Lille 74km. St Omer 39km.
Veurne 21km. Ostende 51km (N1)

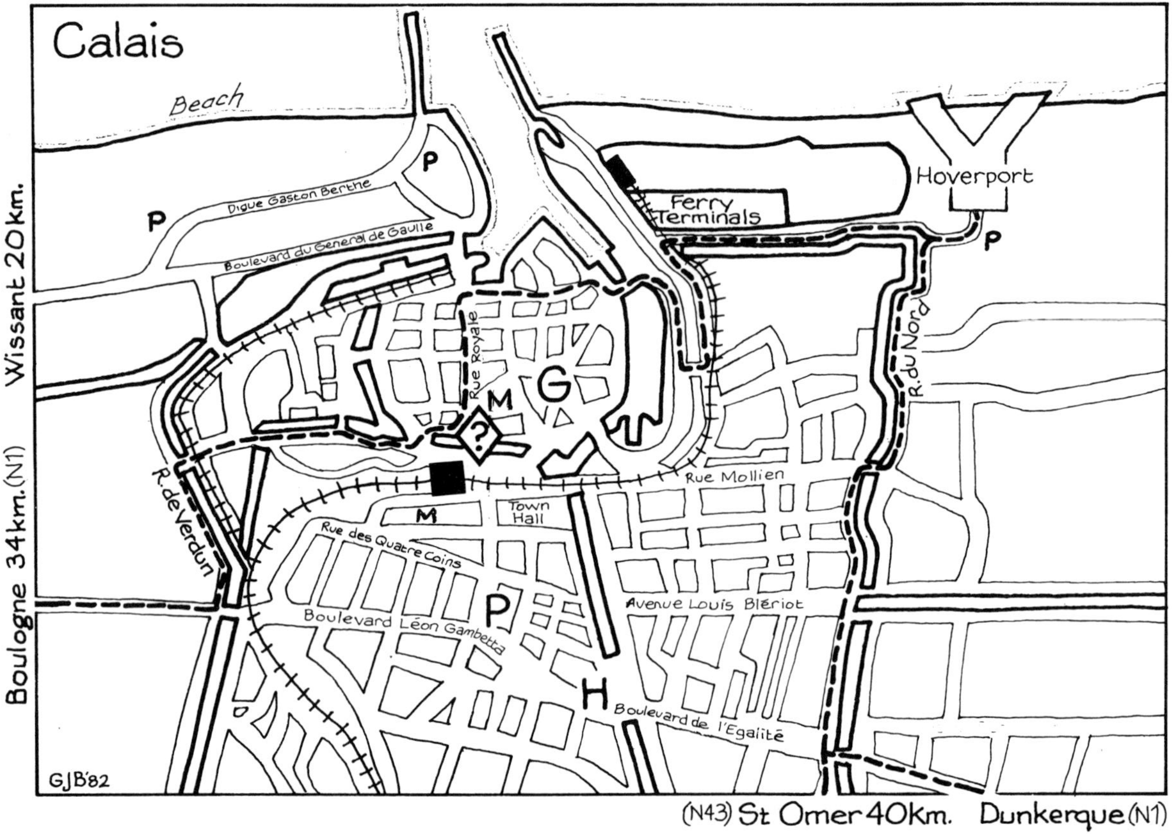
Calais
Beach
Digue Gaston Berthe
Boulevard du Général de Gaulle
Ferry Terminals
Hoverport
R. du Nord
Rue Royale
Rue Mollien
Town Hall
R. de Verdun
Rue des Quatre Coins
Boulevard Léon Gambetta
Avenue Louis Blériot
Boulevard de l'Egalité
GJB'82
Wissant 20km.
Boulogne 34km. (N1)
(N43) St Omer 40Km.
Dunkerque (N1)

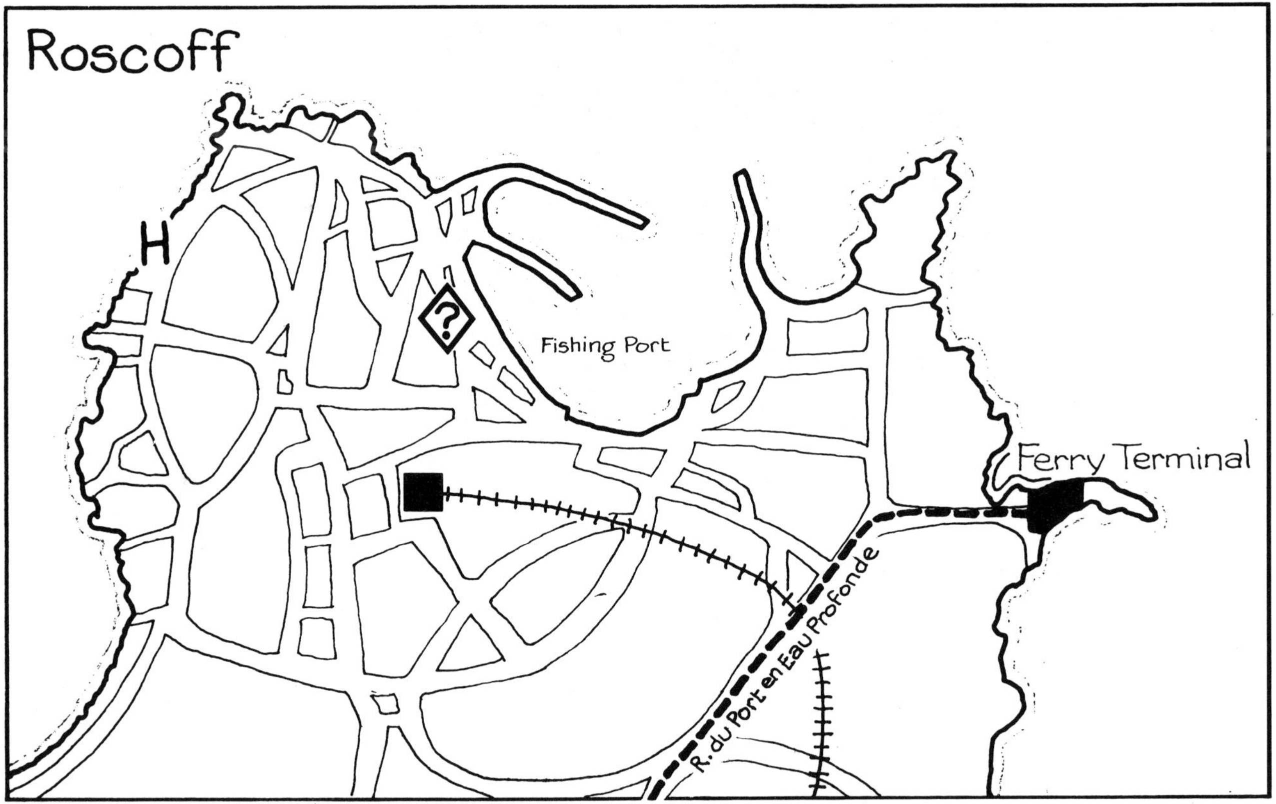

Morlaix 27km. Brest 61km. (D788)

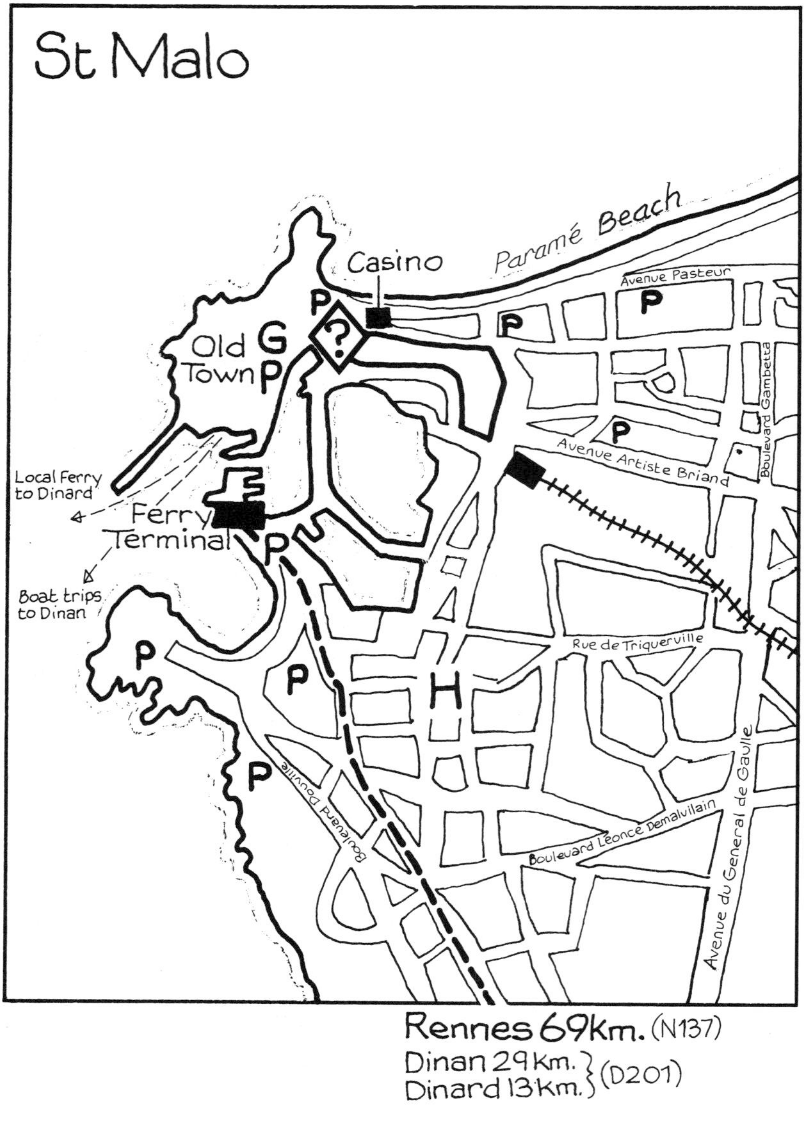

Rennes 69Km. (N137)
Dinan 29 Km.
Dinard 13 Km. } (D201)

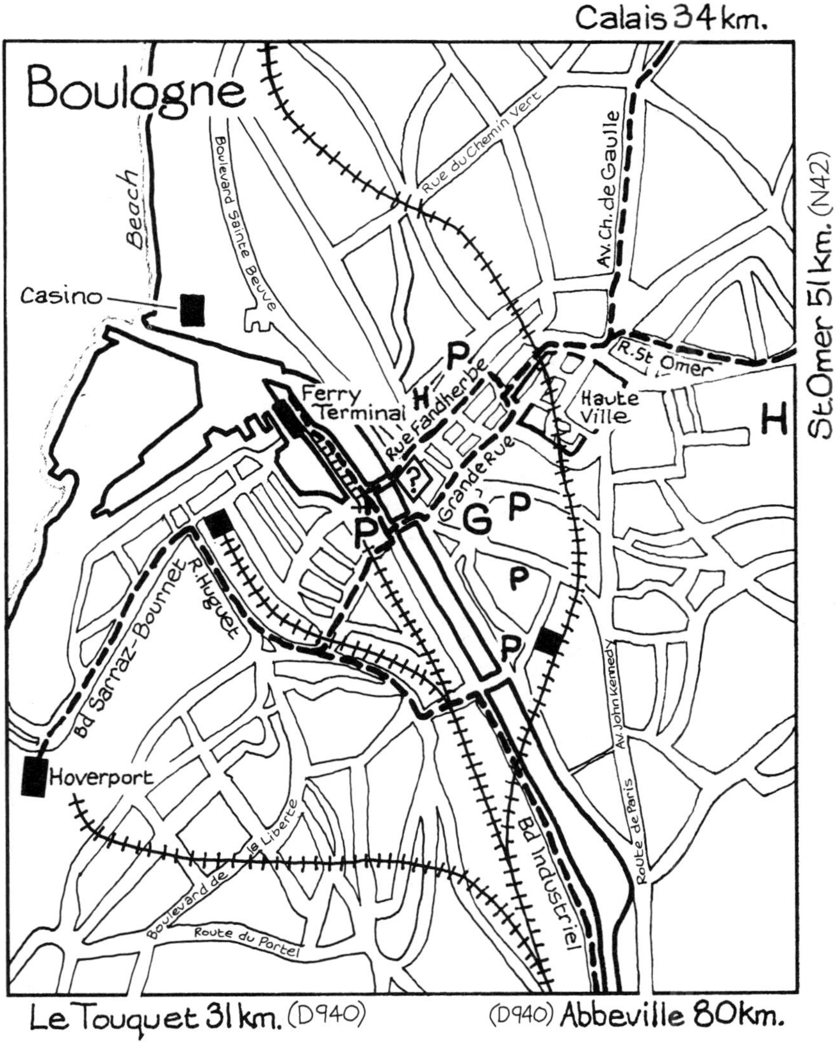
Calais 34 km.
Boulogne
Beach
Casino
Boulevard Sainte Beuve
Rue du Chemin Vert
Av. Ch. de Gaulle
St.Omer 51 km. (N42)
R. St Omer
P
H
Ferry Terminal
Rue Faidherbe
Haute Ville
H
?
Grande Rue
G
P
P
P
P
Bd Sarraz-Bournet
R. Huguet
Hoverport
Av. John Kennedy
Route de Paris
Bd Industriel
Boulevard de la Liberte
Route du Portel
Le Touquet 31 km. (D940)
(D940) Abbeville 80 km.

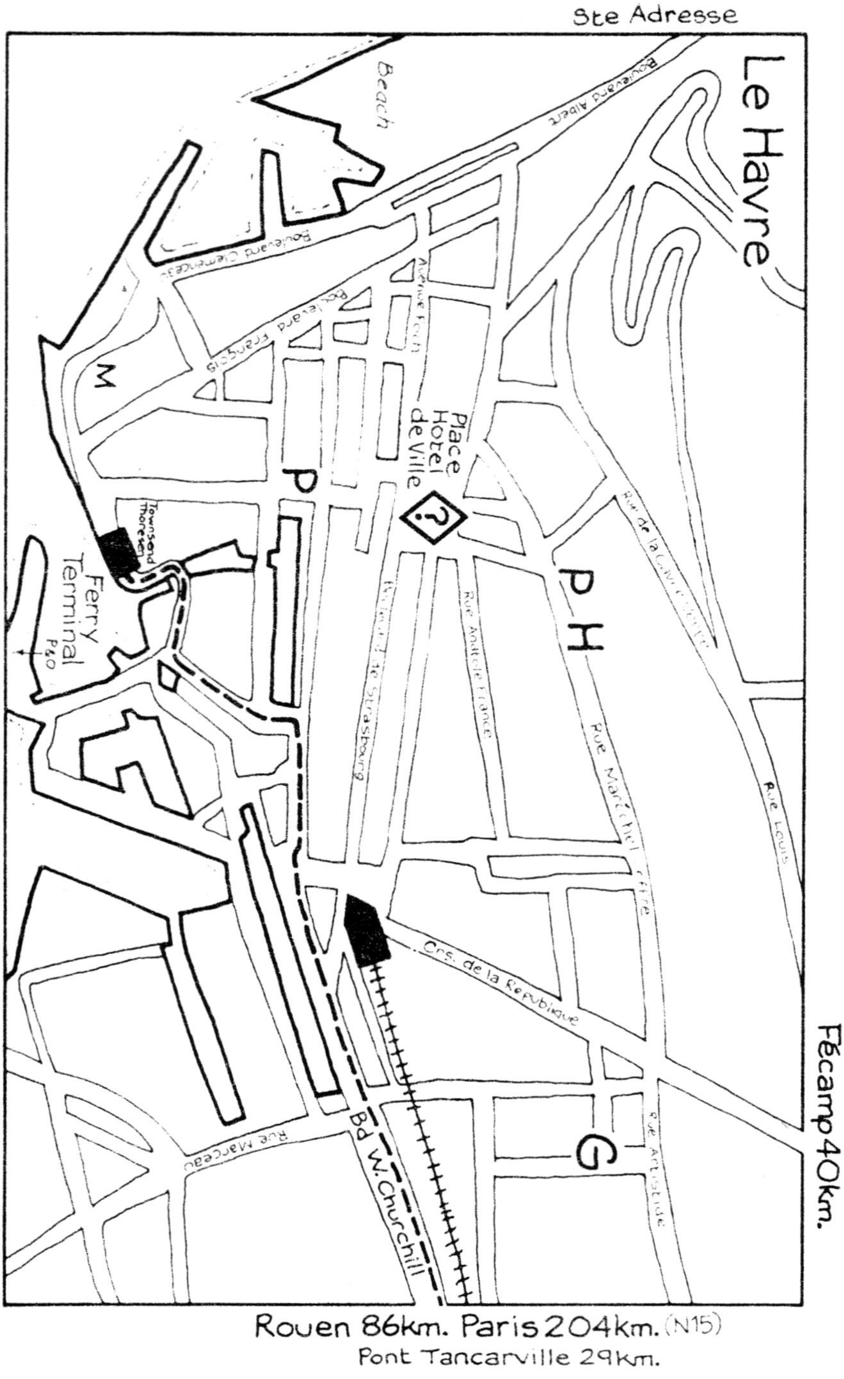
Ste Adresse
Le Havre
Beach
Boulevard Albert
Boulevard Clemenceau
Avenue Foch
Boulevard François
M
Place Hotel de Ville
P
Townsend Thoresen
Ferry Terminal
P&O
P H
Boulevard de Strasbourg
Rue Anatole France
Rue Louis
Crs. de la République
G
Rue Marceau
Bd W. Churchill
Fécamp 40km.
Rouen 86km. Paris 204km. (N15)
Pont Tancarville 29km.

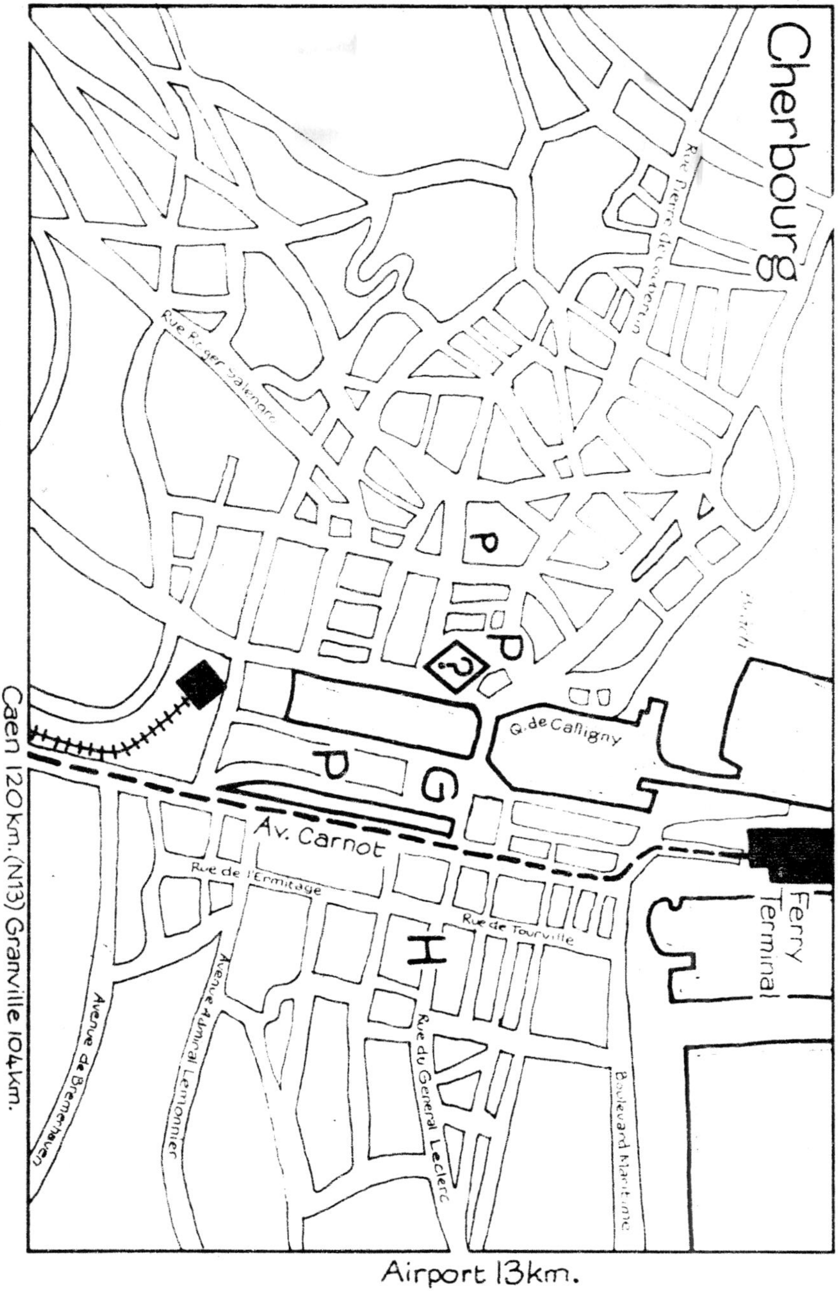

Cherbourg
Rue Pierre de Coubertin
Rue Roger Salengro
P
P
P
G
H
Q. de Caligny
Av. Carnot
Rue de l'Ermitage
Rue de Tourville
Avenue de Bremerhaven
Avenue Amiral Lemonnier
Rue du General Leclerc
Boulevard Maritime
Ferry Terminal
Caen 120 km. (N13) Granville 104km.
Airport 13km.